A Place to Wed

Romantic and exotic
wedding destinations
from around the world

Jane Anderson

A Place to Wed

Romantic and exotic
wedding destinations
from around the world

To my loves, Steve and Scarlett

Published in 2006 by Conran Octopus Limited
a part of Octopus Publishing Group
2–4 Heron Quays, London E14 4JP
www.conran-octopus.co.uk

British Library Cataloguing-in-Publication Data.
A catalogue record for this book is available from
the British Library.

ISBN 1 84091 430 0

Publishing Director: Lorraine Dickey
Editor: Sybella Marlow
Art Director: Jonathan Christie
Designer: Victoria Burley
Picture Research Manager: Liz Boyd
Picture Researcher: Sarah Hopper
Production Manager: Angela Young

Printed in China

Contents

Introduction

We are all a little bit in love with travel, and escaping to foreign climes is often closely associated with romance. While writing this book about 25 stunning locations around the world in which to tie the knot, I kept thinking of the poem 'In Paris With You' by James Fenton that I have loved for years. It explores the conceit that Paris is a byword for love: 'Don't talk to me of love. Let's talk of Paris./I'm in Paris with the slightest thing you do.' My hope in writing this book is that anyone searching for that ultra-special place to say 'I do' will find it here, whether it be an isolated wooden chapel on the west coast of Iceland or a gazebo in the sand on a castaway Fijian island. The 25 locations in this book were all chosen to transport future brides and grooms to worlds far removed from the humdrum routine of daily life.

There are many reasons why marrying overseas is becoming more popular. Heading overseas allows much of the stress to be taken out of a wedding, as all the resorts included here have experienced wedding or events coordinators who organize everything for you — though with your input, naturally, when it comes to choosing everything from bouquets to sunset cruises. Although some couples run away alone for a very intimate wedding, with hotel staff standing in as witnesses, many of the places I have chosen are perfect for taking friends and family along, too.

Weddings abroad have sometimes had a bad press, with images of overheated brides lining up on a beach to say 'I do'. But it doesn't have to be that way, as this book shows. Each chapter presents a truly special place to wed, where an individual experience is created: indeed, some of these resorts go to the lengths of hosting one or two weddings per month, so that there is no chance of any overlap or of guests seeing more than one wedding during their stay. Handy bullet points summarize the best time of year to go; whether civil or religious ceremonies or blessings only are available; and any residency period required. In general, when a religious marriage is referred to this indicates a Christian ceremony; this is not to say that other religions cannot be catered for, however, and couples should enquire accordingly. Although the legal requirements for marrying abroad do vary from country to country, the standard documentation needed usually includes the following:
• Proof of ID, such as original birth certificates and valid ten-year passports.
• Proof of marital status, such as a certified affidavit declaring that there is no lawful impediment or hindrance to marriage.
• If either party is divorced, the decree absolute with a court stamp.
• If either party is widowed, the death certificate of the former spouse and previous marriage certificate.
• If either party has changed their name by deed poll, legal proof of this, stamped and signed by a solicitor. This also applies if a formerly married woman has reverted to her maiden name.

In addition, most countries require that both parties be aged 18 or over, and some demand a blood test. If asked for guidance on the absolute essentials, I would offer the following advice: make sure your names are exactly the same on all documents; start making plans well in advance of your chosen wedding date; and if possible speak to couples who have themselves married in your chosen spot. Above all, this book aims to inspire couples to spend the most important day of their lives in an ultra-special place that will stay with them for ever, a place that will have a symbolic resonance for them, and to which they may choose to return to for anniversaries well into their marriage, or even to revisit to renew their vows.

Cap Juluca, Anguilla

Imagine walking hand in hand along a vast swathe of powdery white-sand beach, fringed by an iridescent Caribbean Sea, to declare 'I do'. When it comes to beach perfection, the tiny island of Anguilla in the British West Indies, just 25 by 5 km (16 by 3 miles), is a strong contender. There are 33 shimmering stretches of sand encircling the island, and one of the very best, Maundays Bay Beach, has Cap Juluca sympathetically woven into its 1,600-m (1-mile) crescent of beach. Standing sentinel beside the lapping surf in the balmy Caribbean air, the resort appears like a Berber prince's white fortress, bouncing endless shimmering reflections back and forth with the equally white sand.

Cap Juluca represents old-school Caribbean luxury, with an endearingly hippy feel thrown in. Flip-flops and kaftans fit the bill perfectly, though they may be of the sequinned variety. There is no state-of-the-art spa (four-hands massages in one's villa are the order of the day), nor any achingly chic contemporary art around the place, though the simple lines of the Moorish architecture give the resort a calm, minimalist edge. Wherever you look, there seems to be a perfect white dome set against a cornflower-blue sky or an archway framing an idyllic ocean view, with the moody mountains of the neighbouring island, St Maarten, in the distance. On an extra-clear day, guests can see 35 miles (56 km) across to the volcanic island of Saba, too. Secluded and sophisticated, life at Cap Juluca moves at an exceedingly gentle, Caribbean pace. Sunbathe on the beach, and a friendly face will appear with a passionfruit sorbet to cool you down. Go for a game of tennis, and the pro will be there to brush up your game on some of the prettiest courts in the Caribbean. Kayaking, snorkelling, windsurfing, water-skiing and sailing are also available, along with a golf driving range across the saltwater lagoon and a croquet lawn.

OPPOSITE: HAND IN HAND ON MAUNDAYS BAY BEACH, ANGUILLA.

BELOW: CAP JULUCA'S MOORISH ARCHITECTURE.

■ BEST TIME OF YEAR TO GO
All year round except February, September, October, and Christmas and New Year.

■ CEREMONIES
Religious and civil.

■ PRE-WEDDING RESIDENCY
Two working days.

10 Cap Juluca, Anguilla

The people behind Cap Juluca have also just opened (in October 2005) a more affordable sister hotel called Kú, meaning 'sacred place' in the native Arawak language. Billed as Anguilla's first affordable-chic, all-suite retreat, it offers a mixture of South Beach-style minimalist cool and the relaxed sophistication of French St Barts. It has the longest bar on Anguilla, stretching down the beach, with barefoot dancing under the stars — perfect for a hen or stag party.

The staff at Cap Juluca make sure that wedding couples and their guests are treated as VIPs. Couples will usually have been in contact with the resort's wedding coordinator before arriving in Anguilla so that any special requests can be met (on such a small island, almost everything has to be imported). The wedding coordinator will also guide couples through the necessary legal procedures. Couples from outside Anguilla may marry under the authority of a special licence that takes approximately two working days to process. Couples wishing to wed on a Saturday will need to arrive on the Wednesday and apply for the licence on Thursday morning. Both parties must present proof of citizenship of their resident country. These documents are the same ones that couples will need to fulfil entry requirements when visiting Anguilla: both passports, or original birth certificates accompanied by photo identification such as a driving licence. If applicable, a divorce or death certificate must be provided. All documents must be in English, and if not they must be translated and notarized. The marriage licence fee must be paid at the

courthouse on completion of the marriage licence. This must be done at least two working days before the ceremony. Two witnesses are required: for couples travelling without family and friends, Cap Juluca can supply witnesses if necessary.

At Cap Juluca civil and religious weddings are conducted by a minister or pastor.

ABOVE: WHITE WEDDING CHAIRS IN THE WHITE SAND.

OPPOSITE: THE COOL AND CALM OF CAP JULUCA'S ENTRANCE.

A SPACIOUS SUITE AT CAP JULUCA.

includes Anglican, Baptist, Church of Christ, Church of God, Lutheran, Methodist, Pentecostal and Seventh-Day Adventist. For a Catholic wedding, three to six months' notice is required. For a civil wedding conducted by a Justice of the Peace, couples must marry at the courthouse.

Wedding receptions are usually held at the laid-back George's Restaurant on the Beach, which can accommodate up to 150 guests. A typical menu starts with lobster and corn chowder, followed by blackened mahi-mahi (a delicate white fish of the area) with pineapple chutney and cassava purée. The beautiful Pimm's Restaurant on Rocky Point has a view right along the beach, and serves French/Asian cuisine for up to 60 guests. Kemia serves global tapas for up to 50 guests, with anything from Lau ca Cambodia (seafood hotpot) to Indian curried chicken on the menu. A marquee that accommodates up to 150 guests can also be set up on the croquet lawn. A steel band, calypso band, DJ or limbo dancer can be called upon to get the party going.

Couples can choose to wed anywhere on the beach. Cap Juluca's wedding coordinator suggests either close to the main house or, for total privacy, at the far end of the beach. There is also a wedding lawn on the sand dune at the western end of the bay, overlooking the beach, the Caribbean Sea and the mountains of St Maarten. The lawn has a gazebo surrounded by flowers, and a wedding arch is decorated with bougainvillea and palm fronds from the resort gardens. Couples can also tie the knot in one of Cap Juluca's restaurants, which include George's on the Beach, Pimm's or Kemia. Villa weddings are, too, popular for those seeking more privacy.

If couples wish to marry in a church and return to Cap Juluca for their reception, the wide range of denominations available

Feet-in-the-sand receptions can be held on the beach, with flares, flowers and hurricane torches. A beach barbecue buffet makes an unusual reception and might include a raw bar station with oysters, crab claws, shrimp cocktail, smoked salmon and tuna carpaccio. For something simple, couples may prefer to choose a cocktails and hors d'oeuvres reception, which can be held on the lawn or beach. Alternatively, couples can take a Champagne sunset cruise, returning for a vintage Champagne dinner in the sand with tiki torches lighting their way.

The resort has 18 two-storey Moorish-style beachfront villas, comprising 58 spacious rooms, including 30 junior suites and seven suites. The rooms all have white-tiled floors, louvred doors, ceiling fans and terraces with stunning sea views. Couples will fall asleep in one another's arms on cloud-like Frette linens and wake up to the smell of frangipani. Bathrooms are palatial, with Bulgari toiletries, and some have semi-alfresco double baths. There are also three- and five-bedroom private pool villas at the end of the resort, which sleep up to six or ten people and work well for small wedding parties who wish to stay together. All have freshwater swimming pools in an enclosed courtyard, private beach access, oceanfront dining terraces and large sitting rooms. Children are also welcomed, and seasonal kids' programmes include nature walks and cookie-filled buckets for the beach. Everything from nannies to kids' sunglasses is to hand here.

A one-man steel band may add a Caribbean touch to the ceremony, or alternatively a guitarist, pianist or saxophonist is also available. Brides may choose from a wide range of bouquet styles, including a cascade or nosegay, using flowers such as roses, calla lilies, hydrangeas, orchids, peonies, tulips and lisianthus. The wedding cake can be anything from chocolate to Anguilla rum fruitcake, and can have two or three tiers. A range of wedding photography and video packages is available from local professional photographers.

Naturally, spa rituals are available before and after the wedding. A Juluca Ritual for Two begins with a basil and mint clay body mask applied with dry Jamu strokes. After showering off, couples soak in a bath of flowers and Jamu essential oils, followed by a drink of fresh mint tea. Cap Juluca has become famous for its 'Mind, Body and Spirit' week, part of a new generation of spa treatments that treat the soul as well as the body: a 'Coming Home' or rebirthing session is just one of the processes recommended to rid the psyche of past angst, which may or may not be an appropriate prelude to a wedding. There are also all the hair and beauty treatments brides could want, and grooms might like to have a gentleman's facial before the big day.

Once all the formalities are over, Anguilla is the perfect place to sit back and relax. Not surprisingly, most activities are focused around the beach and involve a good deal of drinking, eating and dancing. For a spot of culture, visit the local Devonish Art Gallery. It sells carved wooden hearts that make charming love tokens by which to remember your wedding on this most special of islands.

ABOVE TOP: CHILL OUT ON YOUR
PRIVATE BALCONY AT CAP JULUCA.

ABOVE: A BATH FOR TWO WITH VIEWS
OF NEIGHBOURING ISLAND, ST MAARTEN.

For more information
Cap Juluca, Maundays Bay, Anguilla, British West Indies
T: +1 264 4976779
E: info@capjuluca.com
www.capjuluca.com

Anguilla minister T: +1 264 4972377
Magistrate T: +1 264 4973477

Anguilla Tourist Office: www.anguilla-vacation.com

Hayman, Great Barrier Reef, Queensland, Australia

Despite the ubiquitous nature of long-haul travel, there is still an epic quality about a trip to Australia, with a sense of occasion that befits a wedding. This is a land of seductive contrasts, and the Great Barrier Reef is one of its most iconic natural treasures. Tying the knot there is a true adventure. Whether you go to escape the pressures of a family wedding back home, or to be reunited with friends and family in Australia, the island of Hayman, with its Stella Maris Chapel, is a truly beautiful spot that caters well for smaller, low-key weddings.

The Hayman story began in 1866, when it was named in honour of the navigator Thomas Hayman. Several incarnations later, in 1947 the island lease was bought for £10,000 by Sir Reginald Ansett, a pioneer of Australian aviation who had fallen in love with the place. The Royal Hayman Hotel, built in 1950, was opened by the then deputy prime minister of Australia, Sir Arthur Fadden, and quickly became established as one of Australia's favourite honeymoon playgrounds. In the mid-1980s a massive refurbishment programme was undertaken, which involved bringing more than 1,000 palms from the North Queensland coast. Each of the 22 date palms that now form the spectacular avenue of the Formal Garden was transported on a semi-trailer from a vineyard in Swan Hill, Victoria. More than a hectare of marble was used in the flooring of the resort, and antiques, hand-crafted furniture and a superb art collection all went into making this one of the world's top island resorts.

OPPOSITE: A MAGICAL JUNGLE RECEPTION AT HAYMAN ISLAND.

BELOW: FLY BY HELICOPTER TO SEE THIS HEART SHAPED REEF NEAR HAYMAN ISLAND.

■ **BEST TIME OF YEAR TO GO**
Any day of the year except Good Friday, Easter Sunday, Christmas Day, Boxing Day, New Year's Eve or New Year's Day.

■ **CEREMONIES**
Civil or religious (Catholic, Anglican or Uniting).

■ **PRE-WEDDING RESIDENCY**
None required, so if all documents are in order couples can marry as soon as they step off the plane.

Before couples travel to Australia, they must obtain a Notice of Intention to Marry from the Australian High Commission in their country of residence. The document must be signed and witnessed by one of the following: an Australian-registered barrister or solicitor; an Australian-registered, legally qualified medical practitioner; an authorized celebrant in Australia; an Australian diplomatic officer; or an Australian consular officer. Couples must take their passports or another form of identification to the High Commission, and pay a fee of the equivalent of A$10 for each signature witnessed. Once witnessed, the Notice form can be sent direct to the marriage celebrant recommended by Hayman in Australia. The marriage celebrant must

receive the Notice at least one month and a day, and not more than six months, before the date of the wedding. Once couples have decided to wed at Hayman, the Event Services team will contact a celebrant to conduct the ceremony and begin making all the wedding day arrangements. A nonrefundable deposit of A$500 and a signed contract are required to confirm a wedding. The choice of civil or religious ceremony (Catholic, Anglican or Uniting) is made by the couple at the time of booking.

Hayman does not normally allow day visitors on the island, but an exception is made for weddings, with guests being ferried from Shute Harbour, the closest mainland port to the island. There are two boat transfers daily.

The most popular sites for exchanging vows include the Lagoon Lanai, a lush tropical garden backdrop paved by sandstone with a pond and a crystal waterfall near by. The Formal Gardens offer manicured gardens, elegant fountains and magnificent date palms. Coconut Grove is a tropical garden location overlooking Hayman Beach, or couples may choose to marry on the beach itself or on board the resort's white luxury launches or yachts. In addition to the outdoor settings, the beautiful Stella Maris Chapel nestles in the hills with floor-to-ceiling glass walls and expansive verandas to take full advantage of the panoramic views over the resort and Whitsunday Passage. The chapel seats up to 40 guests but is also ideal for smaller weddings. Couples are advised to choose their wedding setting with the help of a wedding coordinator once they have arrived at the resort.

Wedding coordinators will push the boat out for couples and their guests. Couples can be transported to their ceremony in Hayman's elegant 1963 Silver Cloud Rolls-Royce with sumptuous leather interior. A professional photographer can be arranged for the big day, and couples are able to meet him or her before the wedding to discuss any particular wishes. A videomaker is also available. An in-house florist, meanwhile, will create anything from a simple posy to a long-wired bouquet, buttonholes, corsages, headpieces and table arrangements. A picture of the kind of floral requirements desired is appreciated and a minimum of

ABOVE LEFT: DECADENT BATHING AT
HAYMAN'S BEACH VILLA.

ABOVE RIGHT: A HAYMAN ISLAND
ROOM WITH A VIEW.

three weeks' notice is necessary, as flowers are ordered from the mainland. Music at the ceremony and reception can be provided by island musicians and bands. There are also sound systems for those who wish to bring their own music. Hayman's Hair and Beauty Salon offers a variety of beauty treatments and hair styling for men and women. Early booking is recommended for bridal parties and their guests. The Retreat Spa is not to be missed, with many couples' treatments available. For those who do not want a tailormade wedding, Hayman also offers a choice of wedding packages, with a list of optional extras from rosepetal cups to live musicians. The most basic package, 'Essential Wedding', includes a coordination service, ceremony location and set-up, a celebrant or representative and toasting wine.

Wedding receptions can be held at any of the resort's restaurants, including the French-inspired La Fontaine, amid Louis XVI-style furnishings and Waterford crystal chandeliers. Adjoining La Fontaine is a private dining room seating 14, with a domed ceiling painted in 23 carat gold and a 17th-century marble fireplace. The intimate Oriental restaurant features exotic Asian menus and overlooks exquisite Japanese gardens, a ceremonial teahouse and gentle waterfalls, while the lively Italian restaurant, La Trattoria, has rustic timbers and hanging vines. For something more at one with nature, there is the beachfront restaurant Azure, or a small candlelit reception can be arranged on the balcony of the wedding couple's suite. Outdoor dining venues can also be arranged, with a menu to suit. The most popular choices are the spacious Lagoon Lanai or the Formal Gardens, where a single long table is elaborately decorated with candelabras and spectacular formal centrepieces, set with the finest glass and silverware, and lined with chairs covered in white fabric with decorative bows.

For a feet-in-the-sand reception, Hayman Beach or Coconut Beach are favoured. A sumptuous candlelit banquet is served on tables laid with pristine white tablecloths, and for lucky couples the Milky Way will sparkle above. Hayman's pastry chefs will create pretty much any variety of wedding cake desired, be it a traditional fruitcake, croquembouche or mud cake – a dense, rich chocolate cake decorated with white fondant icing and fresh flowers to complement the bridal bouquet.

For accommodation, couples have the choice of 244 rooms, suites, penthouses and a villa, situated in the pool, palm, lagoon and beach wings. Of these, the penthouses are among the most romantic. Each comes with a butler and is themed around a national style, such as French, English, Italian or Greek. Perhaps the most appropriate is the Queensland Penthouse, which reflects the ease of life in the tropics with handmade timber furniture, the vibrant colours of the Great Barrier Reef, colonial collector pieces and a specially commissioned painting by the leading Australian artist Patrick Hockey. The Beach Villa on Hayman Beach, meanwhile, overlooks the Coral Sea and has its own plunge infinity pool, 42" plasma screen television and outdoor rockery shower.

Brides- and grooms-to-be find a chilled bottle of French Champagne and chocolates waiting in their room, and have a choice of pleasures to while away the days. On land there is bush walking, tennis or the celebrated Hayman Pool, a vast expanse of salt water seven times Olympic size. The island's two Blue Pearl Bay beaches are ideal for snorkelling before enjoying a private picnic lunch. Honeymooners can treat themselves to a memorable Sunset Escape speedboat ride to a nearby beach, with a bottle of chilled wine, a cheese platter and rug all provided. On the water couples can hire a dinghy and chase a wave or cruise to Whitehaven Beach for swimming, snorkelling and scuba diving. True romantics can jump in a helicopter to view the amazing coral reef from above, which includes a nearby heart-shaped reef. The romantic Hayman Experience is another option, which starts with a breathtaking cruise, helicopter or seaplane journey from the Great Barrier Reef airport on Hamilton Island across the Whitsunday Passage.

Hayman Island is the perfect spot for couples looking for a relaxed tropical wedding with great Australian hospitality. This is a beautiful resort where calm and crystal-clear waters spill into tropical palm-fringed beaches, which in turn roll into untouched Australian bushland. Be assured, the five-star experience is never far away.

ONE OF THE PRIVATE OUTDOOR POOLS.

For more information
Hayman, Great Barrier Reef
Queensland, 4801 Australia
T: +61 7494 01681
E: mtarry@hayman.com.au   www.hayman.com.au

Tourism Australia: www.australia.com
Australian High Commission (UK) T: +44 (0)20 7379 4334
Australian Federation of Civil Celebrants:
www.civilcelebrants.com.au

Necker Island,
British Virgin Islands

The very notion of tying the knot on a billionaire's private Caribbean island is enough to make most brides go weak at the knees. When the moneyed mogul in question is Sir Richard Branson, you know you're in for a fun wedding with all the stops pulled out. The Virgin entrepreneur was himself married here in 1990, when he flew in to his wedding dangling from a helicopter dressed from head to toe in white.

The British Virgin Islands, known as Nature's Little Secrets, are a well-known resort of choice for wealty yachties. There are four main islands to explore as well as a myriad of smaller isles, including Necker, plus tiny uninhabited ones with wonderful names such as Prickly Pear. The principal island, Tortola, is home to the capital, Road Town, with its colourful buildings, top-notch beaches, hotels and restaurants. Virgin Gorda is perhaps the most widely known island, as it is home to The Baths, a surreal collection of gigantic granite boulders by the shore. This playground of crevices and pools can be explored above and below the sea and changes constantly with the tide.

OPPOSITE: A ROOM FIT FOR A WEDDING NIGHT IN NECKER ISLAND'S GREAT HOUSE.

BELOW: NECKER ISLAND, ONE OF THE BEAUTIFUL BRITISH VIRGIN ISLANDS.

■ BEST TIME OF YEAR TO GO
Beautiful all year round, especially Christmas, but avoid September and October as this is hurricane season.

■ CEREMONIES
Civil ceremonies anywhere on the island.

■ PRE-WEDDING RESIDENCY
Three working days.

With their stunning sunsets, deserted white-sand beaches, gleaming jade waters, feet-in-the-sand beach bars and sophisticated resorts and yacht clubs, the islands all offer romance as a standard ingredient. But Necker's private status makes it an island apart. When Branson discovered it in the late 1970s, it was a barren outcrop. In the late 1960s the famous war photographer Don McCullin and a friend had been marooned here without food or water as a survival test. They lasted 14 days, during which time they chopped down the island's few existing palm trees. Eleven years later, Branson was on business in New York when late one evening he heard in conversation that some of the smaller, uninhabited outer islands in the Britsh Virgin Islands were up for sale. On hearing that a trip would be arranged if he seemed interested in buying one, Branson grabbed

the chance of an all-expenses-paid jaunt, and when a little while later he touched down in the BVIs he was met in splendidly luxurious style with a limo and a helicopter.

'We spent the day looking at the different islands from the air,' says Branson, 'and finally, towards the end of the day, we saw one that looked slightly more hospitable than the others and I indicated to my guide that this was the island I wanted to buy. A brief exchange on price then followed, after which I was whisked back to the helicopter base, where I was left to find my own way back to the airport!'

Two years later, in 1982, the same company approached Branson to say that if he could slightly improve his offer it would now be willing to listen — and so Necker became his.

Almost completely encircled by coral reefs, Necker is just 4 km (2 miles) in circumference, yet is marked by scenic contrasts. Beautiful sandy beaches punctuate jutting headlands, and cactus-studded ridges top sweeping hillsides. An airy Balinese-style house was built on Devil's Hill, looking as if it had grown out of the rock at the apex of the island. Now known as the Great House, it has a fantastic communal dining table, full-size snooker table, comfortable hammocks and floor cushions, plus nooks and crannies with Balinese statues looking out to sea: all places to find your own space and relax as if this were your home.

As soon as couples arrive in the BVIs, they can apply for a marriage licence at the Attorney General's Office on the island of Tortola (a short boat ride from Necker).

The licence takes three days to process, and once granted is valid for three months from the date it is signed. Couples should then go to the Registrar's Office to schedule an appointment for the date and time of their wedding. If couples have made an appointment before travelling, they need to confirm it upon arrival. As the Registrar has to travel from Tortola to Necker for the wedding, the couple may have to cover his or her transport costs.

Weddings often take place on the jetty, against a backdrop of the ocean and the island itself, on the palm-fringed Turtle Beach with a backdrop of the Balinese-style houses, at the Beach Pavilion under thatch, or in the Great House. The founder of Virgin Records offers plenty of musical choices, from a calypso band to a string quartet.

LAIDBACK RECEPTIONS AT SUNSET AMONGST NECKER'S BALINESE INSPIRED DÉCOR.

The Branson philosophy of throwing away the rulebook is definitely at work here. Intimate weddings of up to 26 guests are best, with a private house-party atmosphere and everyone staying on the island. For larger wedding parties, there are plenty of five-star resorts just a short boat ride away, such as Biras Creek, Bitter End Yacht Club and Little Dix Bay.

Receptions can be held pretty much anywhere in the resort. Larger parties can spread out barefoot on the beach with a bonfire barbecue. For 26 or less, the Great House is the perfect location for a more formal dinner. Wedding receptions can have a theme, such as Vegas casino, Greek, James Bond or Eighties disco. Couples can make use of the entire island, with events in different spots.

THE GREAT HOUSE LOUNGE IS THE PERFECT PLACE IN WHICH TO RELAX AND HAVE FUN.

After a day of being pampered in Bali Leha, the Necker Island Spa that is built into a cliff overlooking the sea and offers delights such as an aloe and mint wrap (using ingredients freshly picked from just outside the door), the bride may be picked up in her bridal carriage — a golf cart decked out with flowers and ribbons. Richard Branson has even been known to sail brides on his hobie cat to their wedding on Turtle Beach.

The beauty of getting married on Necker is that anything goes. The staff will do their utmost to make weddings here the ultimate in special days, from setting the ceremony on a clifftop overlooking the sea to creating firework displays or letting off hundreds of balloons. There is an amazing energy and sense of fun to this place.

For fun and games, a floating sushi bar can be set up in the beach pool, served by the Necker chefs: for this a canoe is filled with ice, decorated with leaves and flowers and topped off with sushi and sake. For a more laid-back wedding party, a floating shooters bar is similarly sybaritic, with staff serving shots from the decorated floating canoe in the pool, and plenty of pool games.

Days at Necker are totally tailormade. Every morning at breakfast, staff will ask everyone what they would like to do, from waterskiing to playing on the aqua trampoline, lazing by the thatched Crocodile Pavilion and stunning pool, or playing a game of tennis (in 1997 Andre Agassi brought his new bride Brooke Shields here).

The Great House has a total of ten luxurious bedrooms, including a Master Suite with rooftop terrace and Jacuzzi, ideal for a bride and groom to entertain their guests. For extra privacy and ultimate romance, three authentic one-bedroom Balinese houses are dotted around the island, named Bali Hi, Bali Lo and (the most recently created) Bali Cliff, which is built into the cliff with an open-air bathroom over the sea. Couples can lie in bed listening to the waves crashing beneath them. Bali Hi has a meditation room and spacious lounge area with CD player and television for late-night lounging. Bali Lo is the most secluded, with its own private swimming pool and elevated meditation room with panoramic island and sea views. They are all wonderful places for both late-night parties and preparing for a wedding.

Branson's initial aim was to build a home there that could be used by his family and friends for holidays, while keeping the island as unspoilt as possible. That same philosophy of treating visitors as his personal guests on his private island is still very much apparent. When newlyweds escape to their chosen room, they will find their bed scattered with petals, and chilled Champagne awaiting them on the balcony. And of course there's no long flight before waking up in the perfect honeymoon spot.

The British Virgin Islands are best explored by yacht. Even if neither of you are sailors, you can lie back and let a chartered crew do all the work. Sunsail (0870-777 0313, www.sunsail.com) is a great company to book a luxury crewed yacht charter which will take you to the most romantic spots.

BALI LO: THE ULTIMATE IN PRIVACY ON NECKER ISLAND.

For more information
Limited Edition by Virgin
Voyager House, 5 The Lanchesters
162–164 Fulham Palace Road, London W6 9ER, UK
T: +44 (0)20 8600 0430 (UK and France); +1 732 473 9982 (US)
E: enquiries@limitededition.virgin.co.uk
www.neckerisland.com

The British Virgin Islands Tourist Board:
www.bvitouristboard.com

Fairmont Banff Springs,
Alberta, Canada

The Fairmont Banff Springs rises out of the Canadian Rocky Mountains like a great gothic castle. Lording it above the fir trees, its towers and turrets are part fairytale, part Scottish baronial domain, both transported to the Canadian wilderness. For a traditional winter wedding venue you won't find anywhere much more dramatic. Couples can wed at the hotel or head to the slopes for more snowy vows. Some are helicoptered to a deserted mountain peak to say 'I do' in virgin snow, before returning to the hotel for the celebrations. Superactive couples have even been known to squeeze in a spot of dog-sledding on their big day. In summer, weddings can be held outdoors against the backdrop of the breathtaking mountain scenery.

Located in Banff National Park, the town of Banff sits along the raging Bow River in the heart of the Canadian Rockies. This is one of the most revered ski and snowboarding spots in the world, yet the queues at the snow lifts are virtually nonexistent by European standards. A gondola ride up the side of the mountain gives nature and snow enthusiasts a clear and safe view of the grizzly bears, elk and bighorn sheep that make their home in the alpine forests.

OPPOSITE: THE BOW VALLEY TERRACE AT THE FAIRMONT BANFF SPRINGS PROVIDES A SPECTACULAR BACKDROP FOR ROCKY MOUNTAIN VOWS.

BELOW: THE FAIRMONT BANFF SPRINGS LIVES UP TO ITS NICKNAME OF THE CASTLE IN THE ROCKIES.

■ **BEST TIME OF YEAR TO GO**
Winter (November to March) is most popular for weddings, but summer (May to September) is equally stunning.

■ **CEREMONIES**
Civil or religious.

■ **PRE-WEDDING RESIDENCY**
None, but couples must register their wedding at an Alberta register office.

Snowmobiling, ice walks, ice fishing, sleigh rides and snowshoeing are just some of the winter sports on offer, perfect for activity-seeking couples. In summer, meanwhile, this is superb hiking country. Banff is also renowned for the warm, mineral-rich waters of its famous hot springs, which help to soothe tensions away.

William Van Horne, former general manager of the Canadian Pacific Railway, is credited with recognizing the potential of Banff's natural hot springs. In 1886 he commissioned the successful architect Bruce Price to draw up plans for a hotel to be built above the confluence of the Bow and Spray Rivers, overlooking the beautiful Bow Valley. Construction began in 1887 and the hotel officially opened on 1 June 1888. Castle & Son Manufacturing of Montreal made some of the original furniture, in the form of exact replicas of original designs from European castles and manor houses. The hotel was declared a historical site by the Sites and Monuments Board of Canada, and today offers couples a combination of grand opulence and seclusion in an awe-inspiring mountain setting.

As everyone who has visited Banff will tell you, the people here are warm and friendly. They love where they live and this is reflected in their attitude to visitors, which makes the stressful business of arranging a wedding much easier.

Both civil and religious weddings are available. For a civil or simple Christian ceremony, the couple must obtain a marriage licence, which requires stepping into a register office in the province of Alberta and signing in person as well as showing proof of identity. A marriage licence can be purchased in Banff at the Banff Bureau on Bear Street (tel: +1 403 7622177). The licence is valid for three months from the date of issue, and couples may be married on the same day if all documentation is in order. Couples from outside the province can arrange their marriage licence in advance through the Banff Bureau. There are no blood tests or minimum stay requirements in Alberta. Most religious denominations in the area also allow foreigners to wed in

their places of worship. In this case, couples need to speak directly to a representative at the place of worship in order to find out if there are any pre-marital courses they need to take or other requirements. The Fairmont Banff Springs website has a comprehensive list of local church contacts, from Anglican to United Reformed.

The 'Castle in the Rockies', as the hotel is known, adapts itself to any size of wedding, whether it be just the bride and groom or the wedding couple plus 250 guests. There is a choice of six rooms plus the Bow Valley Terrace, which is outdoors with amazing views but available only from May to September. The hotel will only host ceremonies accompanied by a food and beverage function, for which there is a choice of

eight rooms, including two marble ballrooms for weddings of more than 220 guests. For intimate weddings, which is the case for many couples coming from overseas, the Strathcona Room is a popular choice, as it is in the old part of the hotel and has an authentic castle feel. It holds some 10 people. The hotel's 12 restaurants and lounges can also be used for weddings.

Receptions can be ultra-traditional with white table linen and china, and a gift table, guestbook table and cake table. Most couples who wed in the snowy months play on the theme of a winter wonderland. One recent wedding had a welcome party at the hotel's skating rink. The couple rented skates for everyone, served hot chocolate and had guests roasting marshmallows at the fire.

ABOVE LEFT: COUPLES CAN WED HALFWAY THROUGH A HORSE-DRAWN SLEIGH RIDE.

ABOVE RIGHT: THERE ARE PLENTY OF ROMANTIC PLACES TO STEEL A KISS IN THIS VAST HOTEL.

OPPOSITE: MANY ROOMS HAVE AN AUTHENTIC CASTLE FEEL FOR SAYING 'I DO'.

Although most wear ski suits, it has been known for some to wear full bridal dress and tuxedo. For a more Canadian theme, Native readings may be used in the ceremony. For summer weddings, some couples incorporate a maple-leaf motif into their decor or create a mountain theme using pine cones and evergreens. Tables may be named after local mountains, and bonbonnières can be containers of maple syrup, a chocolate in the shape of a bear claw, or a book of pictures of the area.

Before and after the wedding, the Fairmont's Willow Stream Spa offers couples the chance to both prepare and unwind. The trump card here, as with everything at Banff Springs, is the spa's setting. Couples can bathe in the outdoor hot springs and watch the sun set over miles of snowcapped mountains. A de luxe suite offers simultaneous massage treatments. The spa also specializes in bridal hair and make-up.

Among the 770 guest rooms in this hotel, couples can request a cosy room tucked away in a quiet corner or, at the other end of the spectrum, an ostentatious suite with sweeping mountain views. If guests are staying at the hotel too, there is no need to worry about everyone being on top of one another. The honeymoon suites are split-level rooms with staircases, some of them spiral. Couples with cash to flash, meanwhile, may opt for the Presidential Suite, with its split-level living room with woodburning fireplace, grand piano, library and a breathtaking 360-degree view of the Spray and Bow River Valleys.

ABOVE: A PALATIAL BEDROOM COMPLETE WITH MOUNTAIN VIEW AND AN OPEN FIRE.

OPPOSITE: GOTHIC BARONIAL STYLE IN THE HEART OF THE CANADIAN ROCKIES.

A rehearsal dinner was held at the Waldhaus Restaurant with a fondue supper. The wedding itself had a winter theme with all the stationery, from the invitations to the menus, displaying a snowflake design. Rooms were decorated in soft white linens with white chiffon overlays. Silver candelabras formed the table centrepieces, with soft white flowers. The cake also had a snowflake motif and was topped by a snowman and snow-woman bride and groom.

Couples can also wed halfway through a horse-drawn sleigh ride or ski to a favourite spot and take their vows. Traditionally, guests hold up their skis to form an arch for the newlyweds to ski through.

For more information:
Fairmont Banff Springs,
405 Spray Avenue, Banff, Alberta, Canada
T: +1 403 762 2211
E: banffsprings@fairmont.com
www.fairmont.com/banffsprings

Banff wedding coordinator
www.simplicityweddings.com
www.travelalberta.com
www.travelcanada.ca

The Anassa, Cyprus

As the legendary birthplace of Aphrodite, goddess of love, how could Cyprus be anything other than romantic? With its tiny villages, Byzantine churches, remote monasteries, renowned archeological sites, rugged hills, lush forests, olive groves and dramatic coastline, its laid-back Mediterranean atmosphere is intoxicating. One of its most romantic resorts, combining a traditional Cypriot feel with ultra-modern style, is the wonderful Anassa.

The little fishing village of Polis is an hour's drive north of Paphos on Chrysochou Bay, and the 177-room Anassa hotel is built into a hillside outside Polis in the style of a Byzantine village, overlooking a long sandy beach with life-enhancing views of the deep blue Mediterranean Sea. In the far west of Cyprus lies the Akamas Peninsula — an area of outstanding natural beauty with a wild landscape of deep gorges and sandy bays. It is said to have been named after the hero Akamas who returned to Cyprus after the Trojan war and founded the city of Akamanitis.

Anassa means 'queen' in classical Greek, and the hotel lives up to its name. Couples are made to feel like royalty, cocooned in five-star luxury, yet there is a relaxed and homely feel to the place that is wonderful for family weddings. The entrance to the hotel is lined with stunning low marble water channels and mini-fountains, so all that couples hear is the gentle lapping of water — peaceful enough to calm any pre-wedding nerves. Inside, long marble corridors are punctuated with stylish sculptures. Most of the spacious bedrooms are in three clusters of whitewashed houses, and have wooden floors, high white ceilings, rattan furniture, plump cream-coloured cushions, billowing muslin drapes around a four-poster bed, and louvred doors leading on to a balcony overlooking the sea. If you have your wedding here, you are offered a room upgrade when available.

OPPOSITE: THE ANASSA'S BYZANTINE-STYLE CHURCH, AGIA ATHANASIA.

BELOW: SWEEPING STAIRCASES ARE PERFECT FOR WEDDING PHOTOGRAPHS.

■ BEST TIME OF YEAR TO GO
May to October.

■ CEREMONIES
Greek Orthodox, Anglican and Catholic
weddings plus nondenominational blessings.

■ PRE-WEDDING RESIDENCY
Five working days.

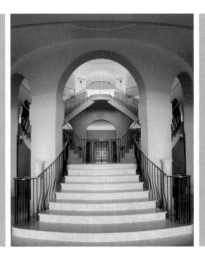

The shining star of Anassa, as far as many wedding couples are concerned, is the small but perfectly formed Byzantine-style church, Agia Athanasia. Standing in the hotel's fragrant gardens, surrounded by herbs, lavender, jasmine and olive and eucalyptus trees, it can be reserved for a church wedding ceremony or a blessing. With its pristine white exterior, simple belltower and perfect domed roof against the azure sky, it could be an ancient chapel, but the game is given away by the modern air conditioning — for which grooms in their formal suits are truly thankful. The church can seat 35 guests and is usually decorated with tapering candles, wedding arches and chair decorations. It is perfect for an intimate wedding, and overseas couples would never feel lost here.

Tying the knot in Cyprus is relatively simple for overseas visitors. Couples must apply to the Marriage Officer of the municipality (area) in which the hotel stands. A marriage can be arranged either by giving notice or by applying for a special licence. Both parties must also present a valid passport, a birth certificate and evidence that they are free to marry. By special licence the marriage can be celebrated within four days, but no later than three months from the date the licence is granted. The Anassa requests that copies of all documents be sent to the wedding coordinator one month in advance. Christian Orthodox, Anglican and Catholic wedding ceremonies can all be conducted at the hotel's Agia Athanasia Church. For a Christian Orthodox wedding, couples should contact their local priest for the licence application.

A Greek Orthodox priest will conduct the wedding in Greek, after a licence is granted and presented to him at least one month before the wedding date. In this case, the couple must apply personally to the Church authorities in Cyprus for permission to marry, and will need to show baptismal and birth certificates, an affidavit from the Greek Orthodox Church that the bride and groom are single, and a civil marriage certificate if either of them is not Greek Orthodox but baptized Christian. For Anglican services, couples are advised to contact the wedding coordinator for this denomination (tel: +357 269 31640; fax: +357 266 13715). The Anglican church representative and clergyman are both located in Paphos, a half-hour drive from the hotel. This is a popular tourist destination and weddings in Paphos are frequent, so there is great demand for this service. Alternatively, Anglican or Catholic couples can wed in either St Paul's or St George's Church in Paphos. Catholics must consult their parish priest and ask him to prepare a Pre-Nuptial Enquiry, which he will send to the local Catholic priest on Cyprus either directly or through the bishop. The priest needs to see the couple before the wedding, and both partners must produce a baptismal certificate and a certificate of freedom to wed. For those who prefer a nondenominational service, a church blessing can be given by a minister who is not bound by any denomination. This is not legally binding, however, and couples must also have a civil wedding at the town hall in Polis.

The hotel's longstanding wedding coordinator, Christiana Mavrommatis, will arrange most things for you in advance.

She goes out of her way to meet the wishes of the bride and groom and has even had a bagpiper at the hotel for a Scottish couple's nuptials.

Cocktail receptions can be held on one of the hotel terraces overlooking the sea, or in the village square. Wedding breakfasts for larger parties are usually served in the Zephyros ballroom, with its sweeping

ABOVE: MUSLIN DRAPED FOUR POSTERS AND SEA VIEW BALCONIES MAKE FOR ROMANTIC WEDDING NIGHTS.

OPPOSITE: DECORATED CHAIRS AND A TRADITIONAL ALTER CREATE A SERENE WEDDING SETTING

LEFT: THE ANASSA'S PANORAMIC
SETTING NEAR THE AKAMAS PENINSULA.

RIGHT: COCKTAIL RECEPTIONS CAN BE
HELD ON SEA VIEW TERRACES.

staircase entrance. Alternatively, tables can be set up in the village square in front of the church for an alfresco reception with an international buffet. The more intimate candlelit Basiliko Restaurant seats up to 40 guests in a vault-like room reached by a separate stone staircase.

Most couples bring family and friends with them. Children are well catered for with the Smiling Dolphin Kiddies' Club and special children's menus. During the wedding a special table can be set up for them.

All wedding menus are tailormade, and Anassa's own farm produces many of the ingredients for the kitchens. Fishermen from the local village of Latchi supply fresh fish daily. A typical wedding menu consists of beef carpaccio 'Oriental style' with spring onion and teriyaki dressing, crispy duck wonton ravioli with chestnut dressing and fresh coriander, steamed fillet

of sea bass with crab springroll on stir-fried vegetables and sweet chilli dressing, and for dessert ginger and lime mousse with caramelized pineapple, blood orange and five-spice jelly. Afterwards, the Galaxias Disco Club can host wedding parties until the early hours of the morning with a DJ or band.

Flowers are organized by the wedding coordinator and are imported from the Netherlands; they must be ordered at least two weeks in advance. Brides usually choose traditional blooms, such as roses, orchids or lilies.

Accommodation for newlyweds is a treat and the Presidential Suites come highly recommended. Named after Aphrodite and Adonis, these top-floor suites have luxurious canopy-covered beds, huge sitting rooms, and private whirlpools on the balcony with a vista of the Akamas Peninsula and the

Neo Chorio village, as well as the ever-present Mediterranean stretching into the distance. After a wedding, a bottle of the house Champagne, Nicolas Feuliatte, is offered to newlyweds in their room.

The Anassa's Thalasso Spa is one of the best in Cyprus, and specializes in marine therapies as well as meditation and yoga. Future brides and grooms are encouraged to set aside a day of indulgence together before their big day. Arriving at the spa at 9.30 am, they are treated to a back massage, an E'Spa mini facial, a manicure or pedicure, an E'Spa hydrotherapy bath, and a light lunch with champagne. In addition, they have use of all the spa facilities, which include an indoor pool, outside Jacuzzi, saunas, steam rooms, gym and thalasso pool. After the wedding, they might like to top up the relaxation with a side-by-side Aroma massage outside – in the gardens or at the beach – with half a bottle of Champagne. There are full beauty services, and brides-to-be can have a trial makeover or hairstyle before the wedding day.

If you are staying in the hotel, you will notice that it covers a large area but is very spread out, so guests never feel on top of one another: it is easy to put up a sunbed away from other people either in the gardens or on the beach. There is plenty to entertain guests here, including scuba diving, boat hire, para-sailing, water-skiing, windsurfing, catamaran sailing, banana-boat and tube rides, and three championship golf courses. But the most fascinating activity is exploring the country: the Anassa will organize a jeep safari to the Akamas Peninsula, a land of mountains, secret valleys and virgin forests, or the Troodos Mountains, where you can gaze down from Mount Olympus. Wine-tasting tours to the Byzantine monastery of Chrysoroyiatissa make a great day out. The hotel has its own yacht and smaller boats, which are available for private hire, or couples can go on organized evening cruises, stopping off in secluded coves for swimming and bubbly.

Occasionally, couples choose to have a cocktail reception on a catamaran, or simply take a sunset cruise for two with Champagne. Those who have run away together to tie the knot alone may wish to have a private dinner on the balcony of their room or dine in the Basiliko restaurant. Alternatively, couples can sail away into married life by hiring the Anassa's sailing yacht. An informal dinner on board, watching the sun set over the Akamas Peninsula where the spirit of Aphrodite is still very much alive, could just be the perfect end to a perfect day.

A TERRACE AND PRIVATE POOL JUST MADE FOR TWO.

For more information
Anassa Resort, P.O. Box 66006
8830 Polis, Cyprus
T: +357 268 88000
E: gserv.anassa@thanoshotels.com
www.thanoshotels.com

Anassa Wedding Coordinator T: +357 268 88238

Cyprus Tourism Organization:
www.visitcyprus.org.cy

The Grove,
Hertfordshire, England

Christened 'London's country estate', The Grove is a lesson in how to convert a neglected 18th-century mansion into a contemporary hotel with wit and flair. Set in 120 hectares (300 acres) of woodland, wetland and parkland in Chandler's Cross, Hertfordshire, just a 30-minute drive north of central London and 40 minutes from Heathrow Airport, it's a world away from the metropolis in its tranquillity and funky country pleasures. Oh so English yet oh so cosmopolitan, it boasts offbeat design at every turn. Martin Hulbert's award-winning 'groovy grand' interiors include Swarowski crystal-trimmed chairs in the drawing room, blue-glass chandeliers, perspex tables and commissioned works of art by the German Object artist Volker Kuhn. Here antiques fuse with modern art, contemporary sculptures rise from formal gardens and plasma screens hang above marble fireplaces. Who says urban chic can't move to the country?

The Grove has a long history of English entertaining, with a house on the site since 1400. In 1753 it was acquired by the Hon. Thomas Villiers, Earl of Jersey and British Ambassador to France, who subsequently became the Earl of Clarendon. As the Villiers family grew in political stature, so invitations to The Grove house parties became some of the most sought-after in the country. Illustrious guests included Queen Victoria, and it is claimed that the 'weekend in the country' was more or less invented here. Today this tradition is maintained with many spectacular weekend weddings.

OPPOSITE: QUIRKY TOPIARY AND SCULPTURES CREATE A WONDERLAND GARDEN AT THE GROVE.

BELOW: THE GROVE HAS HOSTED SPLENDID OCCASIONS SINCE THE 18TH CENTURY.

■ BEST TIME OF YEAR TO GO
Beautiful in all seasons.

■ CEREMONIES
Civil ceremonies can be conducted at the hotel.

■ PRE-WEDDING RESIDENCY
Seven days' UK residency followed by 16 days' notice.

Weekends in June to September are the most popular times and must be booked at least 18 months in advance.

Under English law couples must both live in the registration district for at least seven days before giving notice of marriage. For this, couples must visit Watford Register Office (tel: 01923 231302). It is a legal requirement to give notice of marriage, and once given your notices of marriage are displayed on a notice board at the Register Office for 16 days. If you give notice on 1 July, for example, the earliest you can wed is 17 July. US citizens and others subject to immigration control will not be able to give notice of marriage unless they have an entry clearance granted expressly for the purpose of marriage in the UK, obtainable from the British Embassy or High Commission in their country. Alternatively, US citizens may have written permission from the Secretary of State to marry in the UK, which can be obtained from the Immigration and Nationality Department.

A registrar will come out to The Grove to conduct the ceremony. For small and intimate weddings, the Garden Room in the Mansion makes the perfect setting. Accommodating just 22 guests, this beautiful 17th-century room interconnects with the library and has a large fireplace, funky chandelier and graceful french windows opening on to the formal gardens. Larger ceremonies are held in either the Cinnamon Suite, which holds up to 70 guests for a wedding, or the Ivory Suite, which has room for 120 guests for a ceremony or up to 80 for a banquet with dancing. It also has its own private entrance and reception area, and its terrace is a

ABOVE: SUBLIME WEDDING TABLE DÉCOR FROM RECOMMENDED FLORIST, MCQUEENS.

OPPOSITE: GRAND INTERIORS BLEND TRADITION WITH MODERN ART.

The beauty of The Grove as a wedding venue lies in its combination of classic country house calm with sharp contemporary style and endless pampering. With perspex four-poster beds sporting ostrich plumes, a championship golf course on which Hugh Grant plays and in a converted stable block the spectacular Sequoia Spa that attracts Victoria Beckham, The Grove creates a fine English wedding experience with panache and a modern twist. All wedding ceremonies at The Grove are civil and tailormade by the hotel's dedicated events managers.

superb space for a reception overlooking the formal gardens. For larger weddings, the Amber Suite can accommodate a banquet for up to 450 with a dance floor. Its elegant terrace overlooks the surrounding parkland. For a show-stopping wedding (and the ultimate in extravagance), The Grove will transform its walled garden, complete with croquet lawn and outdoor pool, into a wedding wonderland on a theme such as a traditional English tea party. For a classic English wedding, a string quartet serenades the guests at the reception, or live bands and discos are also available. During the reception toastmasters hold court and jugglers or magicians do the rounds of the tables entertaining the guests. At the other end of the scale, a very tiny wedding reception for just the couple and their witnesses can be arranged in the grounds, where white-covered chairs and pretty flowers make a romantic combination on a warm summer's evening. The Grove also specializes in Jewish wedding blessings, which usually take place in the Sunken Box Garden with kosher catering.

Rock 'n' roll touches include the possibility of arrival or departure by helicopter or limousine — or even by barge, as the Grand Union Canal flows gently through the estate. Spectacular firework displays over the gardens are a popular extra, and for action-packed weddings The Grove can arrange outdoor activities such as clay-pigeon shooting, treasure hunts and archery. If children need to be looked after during the ceremony, Anouska's (Ofsted-registered) Kids' Club takes tots from three months.

Flowers are a constant feature at The Grove with spectacular displays on a daily basis. For weddings, the boat is well and truly pushed out. The hotel recommends McQueens Florists, which creates stunning wedding flowers. Wedding catering is also sublime, with everything from ice bars to sushi stations. Wedding themes can also be requested, such as Harry Potter (when *The Prisoner of Azkhban* was filmed at nearby Leavesden Studios, some of the cast came for rest and recreation at The Grove), Hollywood, a traditional English banquet, A Night at the Opera, Pirates of the Caribbean,

a winter barbecue (heaters are provided) or a summer picnic by the canal. More traditionally, marquees and gazebos can cater for up to 1,500 guests. A favourite setting for a marquee is in the Stables courtyard, which can seat up to 250.

Brides-to-be can visit the Sequoia Spa, which offers more than 80 E'Spa treatments, from facials to holistic body massages. Grooms, meanwhile, may care to indulge in a few rounds of golf on the 18-hole course designed by Kyle Phillips, who explained: 'My goal at The Grove was to create a course embracing the richness and tradition of the great English designs of the early 20th century, whilst accommodating the strategy and dimensions of the modern game.' Or couples could play a round together before both heading to the spa for a relaxing dip in the 22 m (24 yard) black mosaic-tiled pool and sexy Jacuzzi. In the Sequoia Suite double-treatment room, couples can revel in a welcome foot ritual and consultation or an E'Spa oriental joint release or, best of all, indulge in a deep soak together in the suite's king-size bath, surrounded by candles and floating petals. Champagne is of course an optional extra. Alternatively, stressed-out brides-to-be could try The Grove honey wrap, using honey from the hotel's own beehives — a great way to relax and soothe tension and nerves before the big day. Brides will also want to pay a visit to the nail bar, and on the morning of the wedding, hair and make-up artists will perform their magic in the bride's room.

The hotel's 26 rooms in the Mansion are perfect for wedding nights, artfully lacing Victorian exoticism with modern *objet d'arts* and enormous Hitachi flat screen entertainment systems. Here you will find opulent velvet throws, sheer aubergine drapes, cascading glass wall sculptures, and of course those towering perspex four-posters topped with black ostrich feather plumes, set right in the bay window to be sure you wake up to the vista of The Grove's rolling parklands and formal gardens. Couples can unwind with a sybaritic soak for two in the glass-walled bath with The White Company bubbles.

The Grove offers a 50 per cent reduction for wedding couples if the reservation is made well in advance, or alternatively a complimentary West Wing Deluxe bedroom with full English breakfast.

ABOVE LEFT: SPA TREATMENTS BEGIN WITH A SOOTHING FOOT RITUAL.

ABOVE RIGHT: BATHING A DEUX WITH SCENTED CANDLES, CHAMPAGNE AND PARKLAND VIEWS.

OPPOSITE: FRESH ROSE PETALS ADORN DRAPED, FOUR-POSTER BRIDAL BEDS.

For more information
The Grove
Chandler's Cross
Hertfordshire, UK
T: +44 (0)1923 807807
E: info@thegrove.co.uk
www.thegrove.co.uk

English Tourist Board: www.visitengland.com
UK legal requirements: www.statistics.gov.uk

Vatulele Island Resort, Fiji

When lovers dream of fleeing the encumbrances of everyday life and family expectations and running away together to a tropical island for a castaway wedding in the sand, the Fijian island resort of Vatulele (pronounced 'Vah-too-lay-lay') fits the bill to perfection. Here you are guaranteed the warmest of bula, or welcomes.

The Fijian archipelago of around 330 islands lies at the crossroads of the South Pacific. The early Fijians called their home 'Viti', but their South Pacific neighbours, the Tongans, referred to it as 'Fiji', and it was this pronunciation that was adopted by Captain James Cook and gave the islands their modern name. In the days of sailing ships, they were also known as the Cannibal Isles, and were avoided by mariners because of their fierce warriors and treacherous waters. In the age of jumbo jets and global travel, however, the archipelago has become the tourist hub of the South Pacific. More than 85 flights a week land at Nadi on the main island of Viti Levu, which nonetheless remains relatively unspoilt with its mountain rivers and waterfalls, rainforest and palm-fringed beaches. It's just a 30-minute hop by light aircraft to Vatulele, where you genuinely do leave the world behind you.

OPPOSITE: VATULELE ISLAND'S GRAND HONEYMOON BURE, NICKNAMED, THE PINK HOUSE.

BELOW: AN OASIS OF TOTAL ESCAPE WITH NO NEWSPAPERS, TELEPHONES OR TELEVISION.

■ **BEST TIME OF YEAR TO GO**
May to November.

■ **CEREMONIES**
Religious, conducted by a
Methodist (Uniting Church) minister.

■ **PRE-WEDDING RESIDENCY**
Couples must be in Fiji for a total of six days,
and can get married at any time within 28 days
of obtaining the application for a licence.

Located on one of the southernmost islands in the Fijian group, Vatulele is the vision of Emmy award-winning Australian television producer Henry Crawford, who has used his creative talents to conjure up the essence of romance without a hint of commercialism. In keeping with his philosophy of creating an oasis of total escape, there are no money transactions on the island, and telephones, newspapers, radios and televisions are banned. Every aspect of a stay here, including French Champagne, is included in the initial cost, with the exception of scuba diving and massages. The island is similar in shape to a footprint and 32 sq km (12 sq miles) in area, and the 18 villas, or 'bures', of the resort are spread out along a stretch of gleaming white-sand beach, fringed by a turquoise lagoon and set against a jungle backdrop. The only other inhabitants of the island live in four villages. Most of the resort's staff come from these villages, and their natural gentleness and good humour never fail to captivate guests at Vatulele.

Vatulele makes no attempt to offer anything but a thoroughly heartfelt Fijian-style nuptial ceremony, to which the warmth and enthusiasm of the local staff contribute hugely. Once the bride and groom arrive on the main island, they are escorted by a representative of Vatulele Resort to the Register Office in Nadi in order to complete their application for a wedding licence and confirm their single status. A passport, original birth certificates and, if previously married, proof of annulment, divorce or death of former spouse, are needed. The wedding can take place at any time during the 28 days after application for a licence.

Couples must stay in Fiji for a minimum of six days, and Vatulele recommends that they have at least six days before the wedding to acclimatize, get to know everyone and become familiar with the traditions that accompany the big day.

Fijian weddings are based on English law, and are therefore legally binding and recognized worldwide. A wonderfully warm and welcoming Fijian Methodist minister lives on the island and the service used is from the Uniting Church. Catholic or alternative services are not available. The aim at Vatulele is that no guest should ever see more than one wedding ceremony during their stay, so a maximum of three ceremonies a month are performed. Booking well in advance is therefore highly recommended.

There is a real excitement and sense of occasion on the island as a wedding approaches. Once couples have arrived at the resort, they discuss the finer details of the big day with the management, including wedding bouquets — usually made from whatever flowers are in season on the island — and photography. If couples want professional shots, a photographer has to be flown in at extra expense; otherwise they can rely on staff and fellow guests to take pictures. Because Vatulele is such a remote location, most couples also choose members of staff or guests as witnesses rather than bringing friends and family with them. This adds to the real castaway-wedding feel, and is perfect for couples wanting to escape the formal strictures of a white wedding at home.

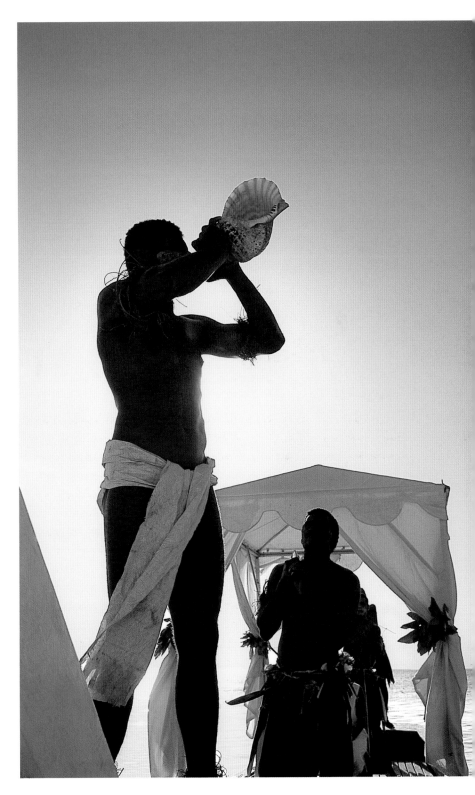

Vatulele accommodates just 38 guests at any one time, so weddings are always intimate. The service is tremendously atmospheric. All ceremonies are held on the beach in front of the resort at sunset. The bride arrives like Cleopatra on a long boat adorned with exotic flowers and palm leaves, under a white awning to protect her from the sun. Fijian warriors in cermonial dress form her escort, to the sound of a conch being blown. The groom waits with the minister, to sounds of the Fijian choir gathered on the beach. The bride is then carried on to the beach, and the ceremony begins under a floral archway constructed from island flowers and palm leaves, with an altar in front. Sometimes the staff really go to town and erect a whole church, complete with windows and a door, all made from plaited

coconut leaves and flowers. The Fijian minister is usually dressed like a British vicar from the waist up, but as this is Fiji, from the waist down he wears a fetching grey sarong and sandals. The ceremony is perfectly timed to end as the sun sets.

Once the couple are man and wife, the island staff will forward the newlyweds' signed documents to the mainland for processing. Copies of the wedding certificate will be mailed to the couple approximately four weeks from this date.

The newlyweds and all the resident guests at Vatulele are then invited to a sumptuous feast on the beach, by the light of the moon and flickering candles and lanterns. The party begins with a kava ceremony, traditionally held to mark any important occasion or to welcome guests to the village. Kava, a root vegetable that looks like yam, is mashed up and mixed with water in a wooden bowl. The elders sit around the bowl and present the visitor or celebrant with a coconut shell that can be filled to 'low tide' or 'high tide'. The liquid tastes like cold milky tea with a hint of cinnamon and is apparently mildly narcotic. After a few bowls, everyone feels happy and relaxed and in the perfect mood for a Meke, or Fijian dancing. The wedding feast is prepared in traditional 'lovo pits', in which the food is cooked in pots underground. (For other occasions, it is worth noting that the cuisine at the resort, ranging from Californian to Thai, Japanese, Australasian and Indian, is internationally renowned.) French Champagne flows, and an informal wedding cake follows. After the big day, newlyweds can hide away like lovebirds in their bure or explore the islands. A perfect Robinson Crusoe day is a trip to the deserted Nookie Nookie Island for a secluded picnic for two.

All the accommodation bures face the Southern Pacific Ocean and are protected by a magnificent barrier reef that forms an extensive lagoon in front of the resort. Spacious and with easy access to the water, each bure has its own stretch of white sand. Doors open on to an expansive terrace, and from the living room you walk up three steps to the bedroom, which features a king-size bed and a dressing area. In addition, an architecturally dramatic, two-storey villa called The Point stands on the highest spot, where it enjoys a commanding view of the lagoon and the entire length of the beach. Although The Point does not have direct access to the beach, it has its own freshwater swimming pool, plunge pool and secluded sundeck. For wedding couples, the ultimate in luxury is to book the much sought-after Grand Honeymoon Bure, added in 2004. Tucked away at the far end of the beach, couples can revel in its idyllic seclusion and be assured of some privacy away from other guests or even friends and family if they are staying in the same resort. Painted a vibrant pink and yellow, this intimate bure has its own private plunge pool and dedicated butler service so you don't even have to venture outside. Known locally as 'Vale Viqi' (pronounced 'varlay vingy') or the 'pink house', it also has its own private courtyard, deck, two indoor and two outdoor showers and a cosy dining area – the perfect honeymoon location.

When the honeymoon is over, so to speak, the Fijians will break into their traditional song of farewell, the 'Isa Lei', which is guaranteed to elicit a tear or two and the promise of an anniversary visit.

FOND FIJIAN FAREWELLS BEFORE DEPARTING BY SEAPLANE.

For more information
Vatulele Island Resort
Fiji
T: +679 672 0300
E: res@vatulele.com
www.vatulele.com

Fiji Tourism: www.bulafiji.com
Turquoise Holidays: www.turquoiseholidays.co.uk

Château de Bagnols, France

The Beaujolais region has a fairytale air to it that makes it perfect for grand rural nuptials. And for those who dream of finding the ultimate French castle, the Château de Bagnols is romance itself. Dating from the 13th century, the golden age of chivalry, it is steeped in history and stands in the heart of this distinguished winemaking area, just 28 km (17 miles) from Lyon and near the picturesque village of Oingt. This part of southeastern France is known as the 'Golden Stone' region, from the local sand-coloured stone that gives the château a kind of historic glow. With its arrow-slit windows and impressive machicolations outlined against a clear blue French sky, it is like an illumination from a medieval tapestry, sprung to life.

The château is privately owned by Lady Hamlyn, who bought it in 1987 and spent four years lavishly restoring it to its former grandeur. More than 400 specialist builders and craftsmen rose to the challenge, while hundreds of specially commissioned items now complement the private collection of antique furnishings inside. One of the traditional manufacturers of Limoges porcelain made the blue-and-white armorial china, the 18th century-style glass was hand-blown in Alsace, the table linen was made in Northern Ireland and the silk for the chair covers comes from Lyon.

OPPOSITE: ENJOY AN ALFRESCO WEDDING LUNCH UNDER ANCIENT LIME TREES.

BELOW: STONE CHERUBS ARE JUST SOME OF THE WONDERFUL DETAILS AT THE CHÂTEAU.

■ **BEST TIME OF YEAR TO GO**
May to September.

■ **CEREMONIES**
Blessings at the château after either a civil ceremony at home or a religious ceremony in the local church.

■ **PRE-WEDDING RESIDENCY**
One month for civil weddings, no residency required for religious weddings.

The legendary hotelier Sir Rocco Forte now manages the château within his luxury hotel chain. The relaxed atmosphere makes it feel like a private home, and if couples have around 50 guests staying for their wedding, they can have the luxury of the whole place exclusively to themselves. The Château de Bagnols opens for Easter every year and closes just after New Year on 2 January. The region is beautiful for celebrations at every season, but summer weddings are truly special as it is the height of romance to have cocktails in the gardens facing the Beaujolais hills.

Nonresidents cannot have a civil wedding in France unless they have been resident in the country for one month before the wedding. Most nonresidents who 'get married' at the château tend to arrange a civil wedding at home before flying out to hold the blessing at Château de Bagnols. Alternatively, it is possible to have a religious wedding in the 15th-century church of St Blaise in the pretty village of Bagnols. The church accommodates up to 70 people and there is no charge, though a donation is welcome. The only obligation is either to come with your own priest, or to visit Bagnols several times

beforehand in order to meet the local priest to make the necessary preparations for the service.

For couples wishing to have a wedding blessing ceremony in the château, the spectacular Grand Salon, with its 17th-century frescoes and Italian Renaissance-style trompe l'oeil decor, accommodates around 70 guests. For alfresco ceremonies, the gardens in front of the château, restored to their 18th-century elegance with a lavender terrace and spectacular views, offer a wonderfully romantic setting.

Wedding receptions can take place in the Salle des Tonneaux, the château's impressive wine cellar, which easily accommodates up to 80 people for drinks and canapés among its rows of 19th-century wine barrels, all illuminated by candlelight. Alternatively, the Cuvage, a huge room containing ancient wine presses where formerly wine was made, makes a spectacular venue. Its decoration

is typical of the region, with a majestic fireplace and wine presses dating from the 15th, 16th and 17th centuries. Candlelit wedding breakfasts for up to 120 guests feature great spit roasts cooked in the huge open fireplace. Other summer alternatives include an alfresco wedding lunch in the garden under the ancient lime trees.

Couples can end their reception with a dramatic firework display to music, or make a memorable exit (or entrance) by hot-air balloon over the château and Beaujolais region, available early morning or evening. A helicopter is also available.

There are also additional wedding services on offer to make the day feel really special, including a horse-drawn carriage to transport the bride and groom to and from the church or to arrive at the château in aristocratic style.

Beautiful floral decorations can be provided either in a country theme with sweet peas, anemones and freesias, or if the couple prefer, more traditional dispalys of ivy and roses. Music plays an important part in creating the special atmosphere here, and the château can arrange a classical quartet with musicians from the Lyon Conservatoire, a pianist and choir, a jazz trio, a rock band or a DJ. Dancing in the inner courtyard can be arranged or guests can be entertained by medieval-style jesters.

The cuisine at the château is of the highest standard: the hotel holds a Michelin star, and Lyon is renowned as the gastronomic centre of France. Regional and seasonal specialities typically available for a wedding feast include lentil and sausage salad, whole suckling pig with a spicy honey glaze, and fruit poached in Beaujolais wine, served chilled with caramel ice cream.

The château has 21 spacious bedrooms and private suites, all individually furnished with hand-picked antiques and silk damask drapes; many also have original wall paintings and four-poster beds. All rooms have very distinctive characteristics; wedding couples might like to request the stunning 18th-century *lit à la Turque*, the Madame de Sévigné Suite with its Mogul-inspired decor, or The Chapel Room where the sumptuous bed with 17th-century columns is set in a charming alcove with wall paintings depicting scenes from the life of St Jerome. The sitting room of the Appartement des Bouquets, meanwhile, boasts stunning Renaissance wall paintings depicting birds and flowers.

A number of the rooms are located in the Résidence, the original stable buildings. These rooms are more rustic in style, though still grand and all having four-poster beds. Room 15 has a private terrace overlooking the valley. All the bathrooms feature luxuriously large baths in which to lie back with your loved one immersed in the heady aroma of the complimentary rich lavender bath essence. For a regal touch, original 'thunder boxes' or WCs are concealed by old-fashioned elaborate thrones or seats which make a memorable feature.

For any bride who has ever dreamed of tying the knot in a medieval castle, Château de Bagnols is the answer. A French country wedding in the grand surroundings of Château de Bagnols is sure to bring alive the age of chivalry in which the castle originated. All that's required, of course, is a damsel and a knight in shining armour — the château will do the rest.

THE PICTURESQUE VILLAGE
OF OINGT LIES NEARBY.

For more information
Château de Bagnols, 69620 Bagnols, France
T: +33 474 714000
E: info@bagnols.com
www.roccofortehotels.com

Church of St Blaise:
www.bagnols.org/gb/EGLISE.php3
French Tourist Board:
www.franceguide.com

Raffles Resort,
Canouan Island, The Grenadines

Tropical palms and bougainvillea have now replaced the oaks and country roses around the 19th-century English country church brought all the way from Canterbury, Kent, to Canouan Island in the Grenadines. Transported to this idyllic island stone by stone and restored by an Italian architect, it makes the perfect wedding venue for those who want a traditional church wedding in an exotic location, with sunshine and breathtaking views of the Caribbean guaranteed.

Unspoiled and relatively undiscovered, Canouan Island is one of the most up-and-coming luxury islands in the Caribbean. Located in the heart of the Grenadines, less than 32 km (20 miles) south of Mustique and 177 km (110 miles) west of Barbados, the 8 sq km (3 sq mile) island is surrounded by secluded bays and coves and one of the world's largest coral reefs, offering incredible diving and snorkelling. The Grenadines are also renowned as one of the finest sailing spots in the Caribbean, so are perfect for couples who wish to honeymoon by island-hopping by private sailing boat.

Raffles Resort is set around the protected bay, with each of the 156 single- and double-storey villas facing out across the blue waters. High on a hill overlooking the northern Grenadines, with sweeping views over the resort and the reef, is the exclusive Villa Monte Carlo — a palatial building that houses a European style casino, a gourmet restaurant and an elegant ballroom for private functions, plus wonderful outdoor terraces.

OPPOSITE: AN ENGLISH COUNTRY CHURCH IN THE HEART OF THE CARIBBEAN.

BELOW: CANOUAN IS PART OF THE ISLAND CHAIN KNOWN AS THE GRENADINES.

■ BEST TIME OF YEAR TO GO
December to March.

■ CEREMONIES
Civil or religious.

■ PRE-WEDDING RESIDENCY
One clear day (not including the day of arrival).

ABOVE: CANOUAN ISLAND'S 19TH
CENTURY CHURCH HOLDS UP TO
200 GUESTS STANDING.

OPPOSITE: FORMAL WHITE WEDDINGS
IN THE LAIDBACK CARIBBEAN.

Thursday ready for their wedding on a Saturday, they would therefore have to arrive in Canouan Island on the Tuesday. Upon arrival on Canouan, all guests are presented with customs and immigration forms, and these are required as proof of residency when applying for a marriage licence. The Governor General's Licence must be obtained at the Ministry of Justice, Kingstown, on the island of St Vincent – Raffles will provide a private taxi-plane for couples to do this.

The wedding ceremony may be civil or religious: the resident Justice of the Peace is also an Anglican priest who can perform services in the church. A number of officiants of other faiths, including Catholic, Fundamental Baptist and Seventh-Day Adventist, are also available among the other islands of St Vincent and the Grenadines and may be able to fly in to Canouan on request. Couples should give as much advance warning to the wedding coordinators before they travel, if they require an officiant of another faith. The marriage licence process in St Vincent usually takes half a day, and afterwards the bride and groom can shop or sightsee in St Vincent until the return taxi-plane back to Canouan, which leaves at 5 pm daily.

The Trump International Golf Club is one of the best in the Caribbean, and tennis, sailing, scuba diving, windsurfing and volleyball are all also available. As this is a private island resort, couples are given personalized support every step of the way. The 'For the Fortunate Two' package even includes a personal assistant in St Vincent (the capital of the Grenadines) to assist with the process of obtaining the marriage licence. The future bride and groom must have a residency of one clear day before applying for the marriage licence. For example, if they want to apply for the licence in St Vincent on a

Every wedding is customized to the couple's wishes, and the amazing setting of the 19th-century church in the middle of the resort is understandably the principal attraction for many brides and grooms. Up to 90 guests seated or 200 standing can be accommodated inside the church, where a red carpet can be laid up the aisle to the altar. Caribbean ginger blooms decorate the courtyard, while flower petals strewn around and tropical flowers on the altar and pew ends make a very romantic setting.

If barefoot chic is more appealing, beach ceremonies are available for up to 200 guests seated or standing on the white sands, with a bridal arch adorned with exotic flowers. Alternatively, couples may choose to wed on the top of Breezy Point at the Villa Monte Carlo Terrace, with panoramic views of the Grenadines for up to 20 guests. The grand villa, styled after a Mediterranean palace, is designed to transport guests back to a time when evening galas were truly grand. For small, intimate weddings for up to eight guests, the Ocean View Palapa has wonderful panoramic views and can be adorned with exotic flowers and palm leaves.

The bride and groom can then be driven from their chosen venue to the reception in one of the island's de luxe golf carts, decorated with palm leaves and bougainvillea. Cocktail wedding receptions are held in Bellini's Bar, where guests can admire its cascading water features, views of the golf course and Mount Royal. Its signature bellini cocktails (fresh peach juice and Champagne) are of course the drink to serve, or perhaps a typically Caribbean Planter's Punch. Alternatively, Godhal's Beach Bar and Grill, built from bamboo and palm trees, is a favourite for receptions for its beautiful views of the sea and the unspoiled coral reefs of Canouan. Another laid-back reception venue is Jambu's Bar, a funky lounge and martini-prosecco bar at the beachfront pool, surrounded by a tranquil water feature.

The outdoor terrace at Villa Monte Carlo is another fabulous reception setting, with the island spread out before you. Next to the Trump Club Privée, a European-style casino, La Varenne, offers superb views of the ocean, the resort and the islands, and its grassy terrace makes a great outdoor setting.

There are many 'bling' aspects to this island resort. Couples can fly to Barbados and then on to Canouan Island in just 50 minutes. A private catamaran will take them round the island from the airport to where the resort lies in Carenage Bay. Hotel check-in is carried out on board, accompanied by caviar and Champagne. Amazingly in the Caribbean climate, ice sculptures can be created for weddings, or wonderful personalized fruit carvings. Wedding cakes range from coconut and passionfruit mousse cake to chocolate pound cake filled with chocolate ganache. Candles and sparklers are also available. The Raffles Resort has wedding coordinators to organize all wedding arrangements in advance.

Designed to resemble the original colonial architecture of Raffles Hotel in Singapore, the spacious rooms of the resort's villas and suites are decorated with custom-made bamboo furnishings, Frette linens on netted four-poster beds and terracotta-tiled floors. Bathrooms have separate glass showers and soaking tubs. There is plenty of room for family and friends to stay, and for smaller parties, everyone can be accommodated under one roof: the new Raffles Villa features three bedrooms, a private fitness area and a beach-front infinity pool.

The Raffles Amrita Spa offers couples the chance to unwind and be pampered, the name 'Amrita' being derived from an ancient Sanskrit legend in which deities searched for Amrita, an elixir that would grant them eternal youth. The treatment rooms are designed like palapas — thatched-roof structures made of palm fronds using the chiqui-chiqui palm from the deep forests of Venezuela. All are built on the hillside, with striking views of the Caribbean. There is also a tree palapa for morning classes of tai chi and meditation. Couples can enjoy a private ocean view treatment suite and relax with the aid of a Jacuzzi, an Asian daybed and a selection of teas. Wedding spa packages for couples include manicure, pedicure, facial and special gift. The superefficient Sugar Palm Kids' Club will cater brilliantly for any children in the party. There is a full-size boxing ring in case things don't work out!

If couples want to sneak away from their wedding party for the night, they can head over to the Tamarind Beach Hotel & Yacht Club, Canouan Island's original hideaway. For barefoot bliss on your first night as a married couple, this is the perfect setting, located close to the island's sailing centre, The Moorings. The 40 hideaways are all panelled with Brazilian walnut wood and have balconies overlooking the Caribbean, with vast, surprisingly comfortable beds and romantic muslin drapes.

With all its many different facets — from 19th-century English church to glitzy casino — Canouan Island is the very thing for couples looking for an undiscovered gem to tie the knot on, in the heart of the Caribbean.

ABOVE TOP: VILLA MONTE CARLO HAS WONDERFUL OUTDOOR TERRACES FOR COCKTAIL RECEPTIONS.

ABOVE: CHARMING THATCHED VILLAS FACE THE TURQUOISE CARIBBEAN SEA.

For more information
Raffles Resort Canouan Island
St Vincent & The Grenadines
West Indies
T: +1 784 4588000
E: info@raffles-canouanisland.com
www.raffles-canouanisland.com

St Vincent & The Grenadines Tourist Board:
www.svgtourism.com

The Peninsula,
Hong Kong

To wed in Hong Kong is to spend one of the most important days of your life in one of the world's most vibrant cities. In this extraordinary metropolis, Western and Hong Kong-Chinese sensibilities complement each other, with a generous hangover of British colonialism. Although there are plans to waive wedding-venue restrictions so couples can wed pretty much wherever a registrar will agree to go, at present the legal part of the wedding must take place in a licensed place of public worship and civil weddings at the Government Wedding Registry. But of course couples can contact local churches for a blessing or have a memorable blessing ceremony at The Peninsula, a hotel that pulls out all the stops.

'The Pen', as it is fondly known, offers couples a yin and yang of old and new, East and West. It opened in 1928, its architects' brief being to create 'the finest hotel east of the Suez'. In the early days The Peninsula's clientele consisted mainly of railway passengers using the Kowloon-Canton station for travel to the Chinese interior, or to Europe via the trans-Siberian route. Today it is Hong Kong's oldest hotel, known as 'the Grande Dame of the Far East', yet it is also one of the most innovative and modern venues in this ever-evolving city.

OPPOSITE: 'THE PEN' AS THE PENINSULA IS FONDLY KNOW, IS THE GRAND DAME OF HONG KONG.

BELOW: A SPECTACULAR SETTING IN KOWLOON LOOKS TOWARDS THE HONG KONG ISLAND SKYLINE.

■ BEST TIME OF YEAR TO GO
October to December, when the city is usually warm and sunny with low humidity. Over the festive period the Christmas lights on the harbour are spectacular.

■ CEREMONIES
Blessings only.

■ PRE-WEDDING RESIDENCY
None.

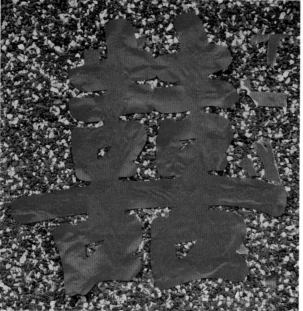

Guests can still take traditional afternoon tea in the lobby of the original building, or dine on Pacific Rim cuisine in the Philippe Starck-designed Felix Restaurant (one of the most photographed restaurants in the world), in its lofty location on the 28th floor of the modern tower extension. Or they can sample one of 25 Chinese teas in the art deco Spring Moon Chinese Restaurant, or have a cocktail and a boogie in the Crazy Box Discotheque.

Situated in Kowloon, the Peninsula commands one of the best vantage points of the Hong Kong skyline, and of busy Victoria Harbour to the south and the cityscape and mountain ranges of Kowloon to the north. The Star Ferry, just a short walk from the Peninsula, goes from the central district of Hong Kong island to Kowloon. Guests can simply sail straight across the harbour into Hong Kong. The spectacular view – an asset shared by the hotel's suites, Felix Restaurant, new spa and even the theatrical men's room on the 28th floor – adds a special dimension to this historic hotel. The Peninsula has long attracted icons from Frank Sinatra and Elizabeth Taylor to Tom Cruise. The photographer Annie Leibovitz's 'Portraits of Peninsula' project, meanwhile, captures the people who make this hotel and its sister properties tick; the faces of pageboys, housekeepers and bellboys are just as compelling as those of her celebrity portraits.

To arrange a wedding in Hong Kong, couples living overseas should write direct to the Hong Kong Marriage and Registration & Records Office for a copy of the Notice of Marriage form. The completed form should be returned to the office by registered airmail as soon as possible. The parties' signatures on the form must be authenticated by a Notary Public of the country where they reside. Payment of the prescribed fee should be made by bank draft payable to The Government of the Hong Kong Special Administrative Region, which should be dispatched together with the completed Notice form. A request for the marriage ceremony date has to be made by letter. The marriage must take place within three months of the date of receipt of the

notice. There is no residency requirement, and the couple may be of any nationality.

For a dramatic hotel like The Peninsula, which thrives on glamour, a wedding is an opportunity to impress. The Garden Suite is a dramatic setting for intimate wedding blessings. Set in one of the wings of the original building, it has the most spectacular terrace overlooking the harbour, where celebration cocktails or dinner can be arranged. It also has a spacious living room with a baby grand piano. The Peninsula Suite is even more vast, with a private balcony to enjoy a full panorama of Hong Kong's harbour from the 26th floor of the tower.

The Peninsula Hong Kong is one of those creative hotels where staff will come up with suggestions that make all the difference to a wedding day. Champagne cocktails can be served in the very hip 1930s aviation-inspired China Clipper Lounge, designed by Denton Corker Marshall, before the couple are whisked off in the twin-engined Aerospatiale Squirrel helicopter for breathtaking aerial views of Hong Kong and its spectacular coastline. This could be followed by a gourmet beach picnic for two (plus personal waiter service) on Tai Long Wan, one of Hong Kong's most secluded and pristine beaches. Located on the northeastern side of Sai Kung at the New Territories, this area is famed for its natural beauty, with woodlands, and mangrove habitats. It is accessible only on foot, from the sea or by air. If the mood takes you, you can take the hotel's 1934 Rolls-Royce Phantom II or one of its

ABOVE: ARRIVE IN STYLE IN THE PENINSULA'S 1934 ROLLS-ROYCE PHANTOM II.

OPPOSITE ABOVE: A WEDDING AT THE PENINSULA IS HIGH ON GLAMOUR.

OPPOSITE BELOW: BRING LUCK ON YOUR BIG DAY WITH THE CHINESE DOUBLE HAPPINESS SYMBOL.

ABOVE: HONG KONG'S NIGHT
LIGHT DISPLAY ENHANCES
NUPTIAL CELEBRATIONS.

OPPOSITE ABOVE: THE STAR FERRY
TAKES COUPLES FROM KOWLOON
TO HONG KONG ISLAND.

OPPOSITE BELOW: THE CHINESE
DRAGON FESTIVAL IS JUST ONE OF
MANY IN THIS CITY OF SPECTACLE.

14 Rolls-Royce Silver Spurs on a tour of the city. To add a Chinese touch, brides can have their wedding dress tailored by Shanghai Tang, which has a store in The Peninsula arcade along with the likes of Manolo Blahnik and Tiffany & Co. Local jeweller Dickson Yewn's Life of Circle pieces evoke Chinese philosophy and the mysticism of yin and yang, and are perfect for wedding rings or romantic gifts.
The name of the funky Chinese homeware store G.O.D. is an acronym in English for 'Goods of Desire', which translates in Cantonese as 'to live better'.

Peninsula staff may bring you the store's double happiness candles, as the double happiness character in Chinese symbolizes great good fortune, especially for weddings. The local Keewah Bakery creates beautiful embroidered satin boxes with double happiness pineapple cakes for good luck — a charming alternative to a bonbonnière. Hong Kong is so small that it is easy to visit all these places and choose exactly what you want, though of course the efficient Peninsula staff are more than happy to source everything for you.

The Peninsula is an influential name in Hong Kong, as it also owns The Repulse Bay and the Peak Tram, both of which make superb locations for wedding blessings and receptions. The Repulse Bay was a hotel in the 1920s where royalty and celebrities from Noël Coward to Marlon Brando found refuge, and it was immortalized in the Hollywood classic, *Love is a Many-Splendored Thing*. It was knocked down in the 1980s, but the Verandah Restaurant and the Reading Room have been rebuilt in authentic 1920s style, with the original fireplace and colonial fans. In front of it lies The Garden, regarded as Hong Kong's finest alfresco venue, with rolling lawns overlooking the South China Sea. The Peak is Hong Kong's number one tourist attraction and is a vantage point above the city with spectacular views of the surrounding skyline, Victoria Harbour, Kowloon, towering skyscrapers and peaceful green hillsides. The Peak Tower is undergoing a multimillion dollar revitalization to create a 'festival market'-style shopping, dining and entertainment complex. Highlights will include traditional Hong Kong-themed shopping areas and 360-degree views over Hong Kong. The historic Peak tram takes visitors 373 m (1,224 ft) to the top and has been in operation since 1888.

Newlyweds planning to spend their honeymoon at The Pen are advised to book one of the Deluxe Harbour View Suites (the Peninsula Suite is simply too vast). These are the cornice suites on the towers, with fabulous harbour views, even from the Jacuzzi. Honeymooners are greeted by a pageboy bearing a big bouquet of flowers, Champagne on ice in the room and a petal-strewn bed. They might like to try out a couple of The Pen's short Academy courses (an hour here or there) in tai chi, dim sum-making, feng shui, reflexology, or even predicting their destiny in the style of ancient Chinese astrologers. If pampering is what they prefer, The Pen continues to keep pace with the rest of the world, opening a truly spectacular spa in conjunction with E'Spa in March 2006. Asian in style, it is designed with 14 treatment rooms and two VIP suites with harbour views.

A major advantage of having a wedding here is that Hong Kong makes a perfect jumping-off point for exploring the rest of Asia and Australia. Whatever couples decide, they will be in good company at The Pen. As the Asian Wall Street Journal noted, 'What attracts the clientele is the clientele.'

For more information
The Peninsula Hong Kong, Salisbury Road
Kowloon, Hong Kong
T: +852 2920 2888
E: pen@peninsula.com   www.peninsula.com

Hong Kong Tourism Board:
www.discoverhongkong.com
Hong Kong Marriage and Registration & Records Office:
www.immd.gov.hk
The Repulse Bay: www.therepulsebay.com

Hotel Budir,
Snaefellsnes Peninsula, Iceland

Being able to walk on a glacier on your summer wedding day and bask in the midnight sun as you party the night away makes Iceland a mind-blowing place in which to tie the knot. Choose a cold clear night between October and March, and you will have the Northern Lights to illuminate your passage to married life. Hotel Budir and its chapel on the south shore of the Snaefellsnes Peninsula, a two-and-a-half-hour drive north from the capital Reykjavik, sit in splendid isolation amid the majesty of nature. On one side are stunning ocean views and a sandy river estuary where seals bask, and on the other the Snaefellsnes Glacier. A moss-clad lava bed that flowed from a shapely crater near by heralds the view of the snow-capped Snaefelsjokull volcano, which lies at the tip of the peninsula. The whole area has recently been awarded national park status and is often described as a microcosm of Iceland, as examples of most of the country's distinctive features can be found here. Writers and artists have long been lured by the solitude and inspirational landscape: Jules Verne chose this remote spot as the setting for his *Journey to the Centre of the Earth*.

Hotel Budir is ranked as one of the best in Iceland, and is certainly the most graceful. Dating back to 1948 and rebuilt after a fire during refurbishment work in 2001, it consists of a pair of three-storey wooden houses linked by low adjoining buildings. Inside, all is clean lines and muted colours to match the landscape. There is an abundance of squashy sofas and soft lighting, framed watercolours of the local birdlife, solid oak cabinets full of precious books, and crackling log fires. Modern minimalist touches such as the padded cream leather seats in the highly acclaimed restaurant are juxtaposed with homely cross-stitch-embroidered tablecloths.

OPPOSITE: THE MINIMALIST WOODEN CHURCH BEFITS THE AWESOME NATURE OF THE SNAEFELLSNES PENINSULA.

BELOW: HOTEL BUDIR LIES BETWEEN THE SNAEFELLSNES GLACIER AND A SANDY RIVER ESTUARY WHERE SEALS BASK IN THE SUNSHINE.

■ **BEST TIME OF YEAR TO GO**
May to September. To experience the midnight sun, visit three weeks either side of 21 June. For a winter wedding, February to April are the best months, as the days start to lengthen and there is more chance of snow. If conditions are right, the Northern Lights can be seen from October to March.

■ **CEREMONIES**
Religious.

■ **PRE-WEDDING RESIDENCY**
None, but one day in Iceland is required to sort out paperwork.

Couples planning to wed at Hotel Budir or the chapel need to contact the local priest at Budir to check availability. For a summer weekend wedding, it is advisable to book up to a year in advance. An application for marriage, or Hjonavigsluskyrsla, must be completed by both parties. This form is available by request from the District Commissioner's Office in Reykjavik. It must be signed by two eligible witnesses who are over the age of 18 and acquainted with the bride and groom, but they do not need to be present at the ceremony. Couples can make use of a specialist tour operator such as Discover the World (www.discover-the-world.co.uk) to request this form for them. In addition, a Non-Impediment to Marriage certificate must be obtained from the couple's local register office. This must be applied for in advance and must be dated within four weeks of the wedding date.

Before couples travel to Iceland and at least two weeks before the wedding date, they must fax the completed Hjonavigsluskyrsla, Non-impediment to Marriage Certificate and both birth certificates to the District Commissioner's Office in Reykjavik. All original certificates must be posted to the District Commissioner's Office to arrive five days before the wedding date. If applicable, divorce and/or death certificates must be faxed to the Ministry of Justice Office two weeks before the wedding date. Once in Iceland, couples need to collect a certificate of approval from the Ministry, which must then be presented to the District Commissioner's Office. Couples should next visit the office in person to present their passports. The District Commissioner will then publish the Examination Certificate, which should be given to the priest at Hotel Budir. After the wedding, the marriage certificate is available from the Register Office.

Weddings are not an everyday event at Hotel Budir, so each one is wholly tailormade and individual. The little wooden church at Budir has room for between 60 and 80 guests, and the local priest, Gudjon Skarphedinsson, takes care of most of the ceremonies and conducts them in English. The state religion in Iceland is Evangelical Lutheran, but all Christian denominations can wed at the church. Alternatively, couples can organize their own priest and wed on the beach. This is such an unusual location that it is a good idea for couples to visit the hotel and chapel before their wedding and plan all the details, and of course the cost, with the manager, Ulfar Thordarson.

A short walk from the hotel brings you to the tiny timber chapel. There has been a church on this site since 1703, and it has a magical quality, especially for a happy occasion such as a wedding.

ABOVE TOP: BEDROOMS COMBINE CONTEMPORARY WITH ICELAND TRADITION.

ABOVE: VIEWS OF THE SNAEFELSJOKULL VOLCANO FROM THE RESTAURANT.

OPPOSITE: THE HOTEL LIVING ROOM.

Hotel Budir, Snaefellsnes Peninsula, Iceland

The current church has a distinctive graphic design, with its black walls and contrasting white windowframes and door, which earned it a place in the Icelandic film *101 Reykjavik*, based on the book by Hallgrimur Helgason.

Couples can enjoy welcome cocktails at the hotel or down on the beach, followed by the wedding ceremony at the church or on the beach with a scattering of rose petals between them to lead the way. Both tend to be very simple affairs. In contrast, the hotel restaurant can seat up to 60 for a wedding and is renowned for its superb Icelandic cooking including unique fish dishes and heavenly desserts thanks to master chef Runar Marvinsson. If the fishermen of Breidafjordur catch plaice during the day, it is served that evening with herbs from the lava bed in Budir. A sample wedding menu might feature a starter of smoked puffin with berry vinaigrette and fresh salad, followed by pan-fried cod with strawberry and chilli balsamico, and Budir Calvados chocolate cake to finish. For a more intimate wedding reception, the Map Room seats just eight.

Afterwards, there is often live music, ranging from a pianist to a local rock band, performed either indoors or outdoors depending on the weather. Dancing goes on well into the night, either in the hotel or down by the tiny harbour, which of course will be bathed in sunlight if you choose to have magical midsummer nuptials.

The hotel has 28 delightful double bedrooms, all decorated in contemporary style. Perhaps the most romantic is Room 25: on the top floor, it has an immense view over the glacier and the lava bed and a balcony overlooking the beach. The bathroom, meanwhile, has a rolltop bath big enough for two. Whichever room they choose, newlyweds will find champagne and flowers to greet them. The cosy, welcoming nature of the Hotel Budir also makes it perfect for family and friends. Although there is usually room for just 56 guests, 10 extra rollaway beds. There is plenty to entertain wedding parties before and after the big day. Guests can go snowmobiling on the Snaefellsnes Glacier, join a superjeep tour, take a whale-watching trip (from June to mid-August to see a host of whales including blue, minke, humpback and the highly endangered northern right whales), or go Icelandic horse trekking. The local horse rental is called Gobbedi gob, which loosely translates as Clippety-clop, and treks follow the beach or the ancient riding tracks of the Budir lava flow. Further afield, the experience of bathing in the vast powder-blue, mineral-rich waters of the Blue Lagoon, set in a field of black basalt lava, is unmissable.

ABOVE: THE LANDSCAPE AROUND
HOTEL BUDIR HAS NATIONAL
PARK STATUS.

OPPOSITE: JUNE AND EARLY JULY ARE
PERFECT FOR MIDNIGHT SUN WEDDINGS.

For more information
Hotel Budir, Budir, Snaefellsnes, 356 Snaefellsbaer, Iceland
T: +354 435 6700   E: ulli@budir.is   www.budir.is

Iceland Tourist Board: www.icetourist.is
District Commissioner's Office, Reykjavik:
T: +354 545 9000, F: +354 552 7340
Ministry of Justice:
T: +354 569 2400, F: +354 562 4870
Register Office, Reykjavik:
T: +354 569 2900, F: +354 569 2949

The Oberoi Rajvilas, Jaipur, India

There is nowhere else on earth like Rajasthan. A marriage blessing here is a kaleidoscopic affair of marigold garlands, 18th-century Shiva temples, Mogul palaces, refreshing masala chai, opulent tented honeymoon suites and some of the warmest people in the world. Jaipur is one of India's most vibrant and exotic cities. Known as the 'Pink City' from the colour of the local sandstone and from the coat of pink colourwash with which its buildings were spruced up in preparation for the visit of Edward, Prince of Wales, in 1876, it is famous for its colourful bazaars and is home to the astonishing Hawa Mahal, or Palace of Winds. Part of a huge palace complex built in 1799, this imposing five-storey pink sandstone façade was designed to allow ladies of the royal harem to view the elegant boulevard below while remaining unobserved. These days the boulevard is a busy thoroughfare swarming with bikes, camels and cabs, and lined with shops selling carpets and dhurries, block-printed fabrics, jooties (Jaipur slippers) of colourfully embroidered camel leather, blue pottery and handmade paper.

The magnificent City Palace Museum, a cluster of splendid former royal palaces and temples, now houses a collection of maharajas' costumes, elephant pearls and weaponry such as the deadly tiger knife. The amazing Jantar Mantar is another unmissable sight. This collection of 'instruments for measuring the harmony of the heavens', built in 1728, is the biggest stone observatory in the world and, though impressively accurate, appears more like a surrealist's playground, with oversized sundials and Pole Star locators.

OPPOSITE: THE OBEROI RAJVILAS REFLECTS THE LIFESTYLE OF THE RAJPUT PRINCES.

BELOW: BRITISH COLONIAL MEETS RAJESTHANI OPULENCE.

■ **BEST TIME OF YEAR TO GO**
November is the ideal month, as the weather
is pleasant and it is believed by the Indians
to be an auspicious time for weddings.

■ **CEREMONIES**
Blessing only by a Hindu pandit (priest);
couples must marry legally at home beforehand.

■ **PRE-WEDDING RESIDENCY**
None.

names — modern-day mogul Bill Clinton was so impressed with his stay here that he came back for a second visit.

Foreigners are not allowed to marry in India unless they are residents of the country. Consequently blessings at Oberoi Rajvilas are purely ceremonial, and couples must be legally married in their own country beforehand. The wedding blessing is highly memorable and moving, nonetheless, as it is based on the traditional Hindu marriage ceremony and is conducted by a Hindu pandit (priest). The Oberoi Rajvilas organizes wedding blessing ceremonies for small parties, usually of not more than 12 to 15 guests. The service it offers both exclusive and flexible: the basic wedding blessing package, which can be modified, includes three nights' accommodation, breakfast served in the room each day, a romantic dinner for two overlooking the 255-year-old Shiva temple accompanied by traditional Indian music and a bottle of French Champagne, and a daily one-hour spa treatment either together or separately.

The Oberoi Spa by Banyan Tree is located in a restored Rajashtani haveli (mansion), with a relaxation area overlooking the glorious landscaped gardens and swimming pool. Its beautiful domed chattris roof is reflected in the Jaipur-blue tiled pool below. There are four spa suites, six treatment rooms and a beauty salon providing a serene experience of relaxation, rejuvenation and pampering with therapies such as massages that incorporate Indian Ayurvedic principles, aromatherapy and Western techniques. On the day of the wedding blessing, the bride

SPEND YOUR FIRST NIGHT IN A LUXURY TENTED ROOM.

The Oberoi Rajvilas lies just outside the city in an oasis of 13 hectares (32 acres) of gardens, pools and fountains, and was designed to reflect the legendary lifestyle of the Rajput princes. Built along the lines of a traditional fort, it has decorated arches, colonnades, pillars, reflective pools, cool interiors and tented canopies with block prints and hand-embroidered fabrics. The hotel's guest list boasts many famous

receives a traditional bridal beauty
treatment known as Solah Shringar. This
includes a sandalwood scrub, a turmeric
skin-purifying body wrap, and a one-hour
Ayurvedic massage followed by Chakra head
and shoulders massage. Brides then step
into a rose bath to relax, and afterwards
henna is applied in intricate patterns to their
hands. Professional assistance with hair and
make-up is also offered. Alternatively couples
can relax by the pool, where guests are
thoroughly pampered with chilled towels,
a banana lassi and SPF 25 suntan lotion.

The wedding blessing ceremony is held in
the old Shiva temple, set ultra-romantically
on a small island that appears to float
among lotus leaves and flowers and is
reached by a little bridge. For blessings,
the temple is decorated with traditional
flowers, such as bright orange marigolds,
and leaves. A flower-dressed horse-drawn
carriage brings the bride to the bridge with
pomp and ceremony. Many couples decide
to wear traditional Indian wedding costumes
and the Oberoi Rajvilas can assist with this
when couples arrive in Jaipur, where there

COOL, ELEGANT INTERIORS ARE
PERFECT FOR WEDDING CELEBRATIONS.

are several stores specializing in bridal saris and traditional style wedding suits for men. At Hindu weddings the bride normally wears either a red bridal sari or a coloured lehenga choli, often with elaborate wedding costume jewellery. The pandit wears a dhoti-kurta, the dhoti being a rectangular piece of cloth, usually white or cream in colour, wrapped in complicated fashion about the waist and legs, and the kurta being a long, usually knee-length, shirt worn over it.

Ceremonies at the Oberoi are conducted in the temple so no 'mandap' (the canopy under which traditional Hindu marriages are blessed) is required. The ceremony involves the reciting of Sanskrit ritual verses, which a member of staff translates for the couple. Instead of the Western exchange of rings, the bride and groom place rose or marigold garlands over each other's necks before exchanging seven sacred vows with a circle of a fire. The Agni, or fire, is very sacred in the Hindu religion as it is considered to be the purifier and the supreme witness of a wedding. The flame of Agni represents the victory of light over darkness, knowledge over ignorance. Located in the middle of the temple, the fire is symbolic and therefore only small, contained in a square metal dish about the size of a plant pot. After the ceremony, photographs can be taken in and around the temple and the stunning gardens, and an intimate dinner for two overlooking the temple can be served.

DARING BRIDES CAN ARRIVE BY TRADITIONALLY PAINTED ELEPHANT.

Larger parties might like to head to the Surya Mahal courtyard, where they can dine under the stars and be entertained just as the Rajput princes were with live sitar music and traditional dancing.

There are just three private villas at the hotel, offering the most heavenly accommodation for honeymooners. Each has a private swimming pool that is heated during November to January, a bedroom with a king-size four-poster bed, a dressing room with walk-in closet, and a personal bar and DVD and CD players for romantic music. The en suite marble bathroom has a double vanity counter, sunken bath and separate shower overlooking a private walled garden. Villas also have a separate living room, a pantry and an outdoor dining pavilion overlooking the pool. Alternatively, couples can choose to stay in one of the hotel's 14 luxury tented rooms with Burma teak floors, Edwardian-style claw-foot bathtubs and simple but sumptuous embroidered internal canopies. Air conditioning and room service make this the most pampered form of camping around. In the evening the hotel team gets together to create an mood of romance in the room, with dimmed lights, perfume filling the air, instrumental music adding to the feeling of intimacy, and the sunken marble bathtub surrounded by candles.

Although newlyweds will be happy to relax at the hotel, it would be a crime not to explore Rajasthan. The very best way to see the Rajasthani countryside is on horseback, which can be arranged by the Oberoi Rajvilas. For a more traditional trek through the countryside, newlyweds may also opt for a memorable elephant safari, followed by an intimate picnic below Naila Fort. Amber Fort, just a short drive from Jaipur, is a sight to behold. Couples can ride on elephant back up to the fort with its mirrored palaces and stunning mountain views. Those who come to Jaipur around Easter can enjoy the annual Elephant Fair, with its majestic procession of elephants, camels and horses, elephant polo matches and the famous elephant race. There is even an often-hilarious tug-of-war between elephants and men.

The Oberoi Rajvilas has wonderful sister hotels in the region, which can make a great honeymoon combination. The Oberoi Udaivilas is built in the style of a Mogul palace and overlooks Lake Pichola and the Palaces of Udaipur. For something quite different, the Oberoi Vanyavilas is India's first luxury tented camp where tiger safaris are the main attraction. The Oberoi Amarvilas is the place to stay in Agra, meanwhile, as every room overlooks the Taj Mahal, itself a monument to love, memorably described by the poet Rabindranath Tagore as 'A tear on the face of eternity'.

MARIGOLD GARLANDS ARE
EXCHANGED IN A HINDU WEDDING
BLESSING IN PLACE OF RINGS.

For more information
The Oberoi Rajvilas
Goner Road
Jaipur
Rajasthan 30301
India
T: +91 1412 68 0101
E: gm@oberoi-rajvilas.com
www.oberoihotels.com

India Tourism: www.incredibleindia.org

Ashford Castle,
Co. Mayo, Ireland

For brides dreaming of a Celtic wedding, a celebration in a grandiose Gothic castle with a history stretching back to the 13th century in the glorious west of Ireland is a dream come true. Enlarged in the Gothic Revival style in 1870 by Lord Ardilaun of the Guinness family and set on the shores of Lough Corrib, near Cong in Co. Mayo, Ashford Castle is one of the most prestigious hotels in the country. Just 48 km (30 miles) north of the university town of Galway, with its medieval streets, snug pubs and many Gaelic speakers, and inland from the rugged grandeur of the Connemara National Park, this stately building stands serenely in its magnificent lakeside setting. It was the choice of James Bond actor Pierce Brosnan for his wedding celebrations, and for couples wanting a thoroughly grand affair and a large dash of 007-style glamour — think arriving by helicopter, oak-panelled rooms, Waterford chandeliers, rococo gilt mirrors and sweeping staircases — this is a real gem.

The perfect setting for a large family wedding, the castle can also create an intimate occasion for just the bride and groom. One of the joys of tying the knot here is its sheer grandeur. Guests approach the castle over a great stone bridge, beneath towering walls that cannot fail to impress them with a sense of the long and eventful history of the place. The formal gardens, with their manicured lawns and dramatic fountain laid out by Arthur Sheketon, and the castle's tall square turrets, are equally imposing. Forming a delightful contrast with all this magnificence is the very personal and typically warm Irish welcome that is extended to wedding parties in particular. Indeed, there is a great spirit of romance about the castle.

OPPOSITE: WEDDING GUESTS ARRIVE AT ASHFORD CASTLE THROUGH ITS OLDE-WORLDE STONE GATE.

BELOW: A WARM IRISH WELCOME AWAITS WEDDING PARTIES AT THIS GRAND CASTLE HOTEL.

■ BEST TIME OF YEAR TO GO
June to September has the best weather, though November to April offers better rates and the chance of a winter wonderland wedding.

■ CEREMONIES
Wedding blessings and receptions can be held at the castle. Couples must first be married in either a church or a register office. At the time of writing, Irish law regarding premises licensed for marriage is under review.

■ PRE-WEDDING RESIDENCY
None required for a religious wedding. For a civil ceremony, residency of eight days is required, and the wedding can take place only after another 21 days.

At the time of writing, Irish law is in the process of changing to allow venues such as Ashford Castle to obtain a wedding licence. At present, however, couples must wed in a designated place of worship or in a register office before a blessing at the castle. The General Register Office in Ireland (www.groireland.ie) can provide all relevant information about getting married in Ireland for both Irish and non-Irish citizens and more information can be found under the Reform of Marriage Law Update section. For any type of wedding, couples who want to wed locally must give at least three months' written notification to the Registrar in Co. Mayo. The future bride and groom can either write separately to the Registrar with the names, addresses and dates of birth of the parties to be married, and the name of the church or the place where the marriage will take place, or they can fill in a pre-printed form available from the Registrar. The Registrar will issue both bride and groom with an acknowledgement confirming the date of the receipt of notification, and this must be presented to the priest or local registrar who solemnizes the marriage.

Couples wishing to have a religious ceremony should approach their own minister of the denomination of their choice. Ballintubber Abbey (tel +353 9490 30934) is one of the most popular places for Catholic weddings near Ashford Castle, and is where Pierce Brosnan and Keely Shaye Smith exchanged vows before heading back to the castle for their lavish reception. Anyone can apply to be married here, but overseas (including UK) citizens must bring their own priest with them, as the local priest cannot accommodate all ceremonies. At least three months' notice is required in accordance with the law. Those wanting a civil ceremony in Co. Mayo should telephone the Registrar of Civil Marriages for this district (tel +353 9490 21375). For civil weddings in a register office, couples must stay in the county for a minimum of eight days, and are free to marry after another 21 days. Many couples choose to visit Ireland and then return home before coming back for the wedding. For a church ceremony there is no residency requirement. Alternatively, couples may like to have the legal part of their wedding at home in a register office, then come to Ashford for a blessing and the reception.

The castle has a dedicated wedding coordinator, Monica Feeney, who works closely with couples in the lead-up to the wedding as well as on the day itself. Wonderfully intimate blessings seating up to 10 guests can take place in the Inglenook, a spectacular hand-carved fireplace in the Connaught Room. Or, the blessings can be held in grounds (weather permitting),

where Ashford's full-time florist can create a beautiful setting. Ashford can accommodate two styles of wedding reception, with a maximum of either 40 or 160 guests depending on the restaurant chosen. The George V Room offers classic Irish cuisine and caters for up to 160 guests, while the more intimate Connaught Room serves classic French cuisine and seats up to 40. The George V Room, so-named after a visit by the Prince of Wales and future George V, boasts pristine period decor dating from 1939 and breathtaking views across the river. The Connaught Room has delicate woodcarvings and a beautiful inglenook fireplace. Chef Stephen Matz has created a seasonal tasting menu based on the availability of fresh local produce featuring dishes such as marinated loin of Connemara lamb with tossed leaves and pesto, or guinea fowl with homemade tagliatelle and black truffle jus. Sommelier Robert Bowe, meanwhile, will recommend

wines to suit each course. For a wedding of 160 guests, all 83 rooms must be booked. For smaller wedding receptions, couples and their guests must stay at the castle but do not have to book exclusive use.

To get the reception off to a great start, Irish bagpipers will pipe the guests in. Welcome drinks are usually served in the imposing Oak Hall, and the wedding couple can arrive by wedding car or horse-drawn carriage. After the wedding breakfast, guests can head to the Dungeon Bar for truly memorable Irish craic, to the accompaniment of Irish classics such as 'Danny Boy' played by a pianist, singer, guitarist and harpist.

Brides can prepare for their big day with the help of the health and beauty facilities at the castle. Treatment rooms offer Yon-Ka products designed to balance and restore the skin's energy. Aromatherapy and marine therapy treatments are also available, including massages, wraps and lavish foot spas. A nail clinic takes care of wedding nails, and brides can have a Flash Soleil Sun Kiss treatment if the Irish sun fails to top up their pre-wedding tan. Hair and make-up artists are available on request.

Ashford's 83 rooms and suites stretch the length and breadth of the castle, some with panoramic views of the lough, others overlooking the river and gardens. The grandest is the Presidential Suite, so-named after the visit of American President Ronald Reagan in 1985; perfect for preparing for a wedding, it has a walk-in dressing room and every luxury for a romantic stay, including a huge bed and a Jacuzzi bath. The decor is extremely traditional: there are no designer fads here.

While at Ashford Castle, newlyweds, friends and family can take the opportunity to explore the Connemara National Park, a combination of bogland, lakes and mountains. Visitors also come to catch a glimpse of the famous half-wild Connemara ponies. In summer from the visitors centre at Letterfrack just 64 km (40 miles) away and north of Connemara National Park, guided walks are led by botanists. The blanket bogs and moorlands of Connemara are noted for unusual plants such as St Dabeoc's heath, a pretty heather that grows nowhere else in Ireland or Great Britain. Birdlife is also varied, with hooded crows, peregrines and merlins. For the less adventurous, the pretty village of Cong, on the shores of Lough Corrib just north of Ashford Castle, is well worth exploring. Picturesquely situated between Lough Corrib and Lough Mask is a 12th-century ruined abbey complete with stone carvings and restored cloisters – the most fascinating remains are the Gothic chapter house and the monks' fishing house overhanging the river.

The lough itself is a big draw, with the chance to fish with local anglers for brown trout, salmon, pike, perch and eel. Its waters are dotted with uninhabited islands and surrounded by meadows, reedbeds and wooded shores that are home to swans and coots. There are plenty of secluded spots here for newlyweds to take a Champagne picnic or just enjoy the tranquil views. On Inchagoill, one of the largest islands, stand the ruins of an early Christian monastic settlement and a Romanesque church. Lake cruises can be taken from Galway to Cong to the site of an Iron Age fort. Ashford Castle can also arrange equestrian pursuits, golf, falconry, tennis, clay pigeon shooting, archery, pony and trap tours, bicycle safaris and trail walking. To be sure, newlyweds will take the luck of the Irish with them after a wedding at this most majestic of Irish castles.

THE BEAUTIFUL SHORES OF
LOUGH CORRIB ARE PERFECT
FOR INTIMATE PICNICS.

For more information
Ashford Castle
Cong, Co. Mayo
Ireland
T: +353 92 46003
E: banqueting@ashford.ie
www.ashford.ie

Tourism Ireland: www.tourismireland.com

Villa San Michele,
Florence, Italy

Florence lies in the heart of glorious Tuscany like a Renaissance jewel. The birthplace of Michelangelo, Leonardo da Vinci and Donatello, nestling in the Arno Valley, boasts the greatest art collections of all the Italian cities, magnificent churches and Medici palazzi down medieval streets, and stunning piazzas. Like Miss Honeychurch in E. M. Forster's *A Room With A View*, many visitors find their breath is taken away by this profusion of history, art and culture. The antidote to the overwhelming riches of Florence is of course the green tranquillity of the Tuscan hills. Villa San Michele enjoys the best of both worlds from its commanding position in the hills of Fiesole, with panoramic views over cypress and lemon groves down the Arno Valley to the majestic city below. The Duomo is clearly visible, but there is none of the hubbub of the city in this most picturesque of spots.

Villa San Michele, named after the church of St Michael the Archangel, was built on a site originally occupied by a 15th-century Franciscan monastery. The imposing building that greets visitors today has a façade attributed to Michelangelo and dates from 1600, when the monastery was completely renovated. It remained in the hands of the Franciscans until 1808, when the monastic orders were dissolved by Napoleon, and in 1817 it became a secular building. In 1900 the villa was bought by the New Yorker Henry White Cannon, who landscaped the gardens, erected impressive greenhouses and restored the building in Victorian style, adding wrought-iron gates and a rust-coloured patina to the walls.

OPPOSITE: THE MAJESTIC DUOMO CATHEDRAL DOMINATES THE FLORENCE SKYLINE.

BELOW: VILLA SAN MICHELE'S FAÇADE IS ATTRIBUTED TO RENAISSANCE MAN, MICHELANGELO.

■ BEST TIME OF YEAR TO GO
May, June, September and October, when the weather is not too hot or rainy.

■ CEREMONIES
A civil wedding ceremony must be carried out first in the Palazzo Vecchio, followed by a religious wedding blessing at Villa San Michele. Catholic ceremonies are not possible.

■ PRE-WEDDING RESIDENCY
Couples should allow a month for planning and arrive at least one day before the ceremony. Villa San Michele advises that couples arrive four days before the wedding.

candles had dulled the colours, but restoration work has revealed astonishing details such as an oil lamp above Christ's halo, a small white cat and the identity of Judas — revealed as the only apostle without a halo. The Limonaia is another beautiful part of the hotel. Created by the monks for storing the potted lemon trees during the winter, this historic, high-ceilinged building has been transformed into two panoramic suites, one with a private terrace, the other with a private lawn. The beautiful Loggia runs alongside the main building. This semi-alfresco area, now used for dining, is decorated with huge pots filled with colourful seasonal flowers and offers the most awe-inspiring views over Florence. Outside, the gardens are a profusion of rosemary and lavender, with a century-old wisteria and a graceful, heated outdoor pool with breathtaking views — a truly romantic setting.

NEWLYWEDS OFTEN SPEND THEIR FIRST NIGHT IN THE OLD CHAPEL SUITE.

Henry White Cannon also converted the courtyard into a winter garden. After being severely damaged during the Second World War, the estate was bought in 1982 by Orient-Express Hotels and was carefully renovated into one of the best hotels in the world with the cooperation of the Florence Fine Arts Authority.

If you choose to have your wedding at Villa San Michele, you will be steeped in history. The Last Supper Room, for example, has a fresco completed by Nicodemo Ferrucci in 1642, originally designed to decorate the refectory, as it was then, for the monks. Smoke from the fireplace and

For foreigners wishing to tie the knot here, there is no waiting period and no pre-wedding residency is required. But although the paperwork necessary for a civil wedding ceremony is not terribly difficult to obtain, it is still recommended that you contact a professional wedding coordinator who can more easily and assuredly navigate the byways of Italian bureaucracy and make sure your wedding goes without a hitch. The company that organizes the legalities of weddings at the Villa San Michele is Atlantica Centro Servizi, headed by Elena Giorgetti. Non-Italians will need a passport or a military identification card, and couples will need to bring their birth certificates.

They will also need to provide a sworn statement, prepared in advance and signed by four witnesses, guaranteeing that according to the laws of their country of residence they are legally eligible to marry. They will then need to swear the same thing before an official at their embassy or consulate in Italy. In order to be sure all the paperwork is in place, couples should plan to be at Villa San Michele four days before the planned ceremony to allow enough time for the necessary checks.

Ceremonies held at Villa San Michele are religious, with the option of a full-length service with readings and passages from the Gospel if desired, or a more simple blessing with an exchange of vows, carried out by the Reverend of the Episcopal Church of Florence. This ceremony has no legal validity, however, so couples must first wed in a civil service at the Palazzo Vecchio in Florence, usually in the morning before the religious ceremony in the afternoon. A horse and carriage can be arranged for a romantic journey to a wedding at the Palazzo Vecchio, with a chauffeur-driven car laid on to return to the hotel afterwards.

The hotel is ideal for large, glamorous family weddings in which the celebrations go on for days. One such party lasted three days and included a costumed Renaissance feast at a nearby castle, a Dolce Vita evening, Andrea Boccelli singing Ave Maria, and a 2 m (6 ft) high wedding cake flown in from Paris in a private jet, which took three pâtisserie chefs to assemble! Another wedding had a live concert with a synchronized firework display.

For larger weddings, couples usually have cocktails served in the Italian Gardens after the ceremony, followed by dinner in the Last Supper Room. The Loggia makes an excellent alternative to the Last Supper Room for a lunch reception. Children are

very welcome and a separate table can be set up for them. Menus can be personally designed to couples' requirements with the help of the food and beverage manager. The venues are often decorated with seasonal flowers and fruits: huge sunflowers, pyramids of lemons and oranges entwined with ivy and even strawberries are all popular choices. Live classical music, a pianist, a disco or soft music are all available.

Of course the hotel can also provide low-key weddings for two, often set around the Old Chapel Suite. Situated in the woodlands above the hotel with its own quaint walkway and terrace, the small 17th-century Cappellina was used by the monks as a place for prayer and quiet meditation. Today it has been restored

to make a magnificently romantic place in which to dine à deux and a secluded location in which to spend a very special first night as man and wife.

If the hotel is not booked exclusively for the big day, Villa San Michele can accommodate up to 50 wedding guests. If it is booked exclusively, up to 90 guests can stay at the hotel and a further 20 can stay at the neighbouring Villa Fiesole hotel. Large wedding ceremonies are usually held in the Italian Gardens. For a smaller wedding of up to 15 people, the Garden Suites are recommended for guests, with their intimate atmosphere and wonderful views over Florence.

Newlyweds usually retire to the Old Chapel Suite, which is decorated for the occasion with romantic touches such as rose petals, perfumed candles, flowers and champagne. Scented soaps in the bathroom are by the famous Farmacia di Santa Maria Novella, and their fragrance is sure to remind couples of their wedding night. A romantic dinner for two can be set up on the private terrace of the suite, with a violinist to serenade them.

ABOVE TOP: STUNNING VIEWS OF
FLORENCE OVER THE HILLS OF FIESOLE.

ABOVE: THE LOGGIA OFFERS SEMI
ALFRESCO WEDDING RECEPTIONS.

There is plenty to keep guests entertained here or for newlyweds to do on their honeymoon. Florence oozes with culture and there is a range of things to see and do from admiring the Old Masters in the Uffizi gallery to picking up a bargain in the street markets. In addition to exploring Florence, riding, tennis and golf are all available close by. The hotel can organize a sightseeing trip in a vintage car or a boat trip on the Arno. Day trips can be arranged to the Medici Villas, San Gimignano, Siena and the Tuscan countryside. The Chianti area, between Florence and Siena, is one of the most beautiful in Italy and a famous wine production region. Just south of Florence is the Cappannelle Winery, a sister property of Villa San Michele, where honeymooners can stay in one of just five bedrooms and enjoy the services of their own personal wine butler.

This is a romantic city for a romantic couple and makes a truly beautiful destination for a memorable wedding.

For more information
Villa San Michele, Via Doccia 4,
Fiesole, 50014 Florence, Italy
T: +39 055 5678200
E: reservations@villasanmichele.net
www.villasanmichele.com

Atlantica Centro Servizi:
T: +39 055 6235924 F: +39 055 6236293
E: info@atlantica-service.it
Italian Tourist Board: www.italiantouristboard.co.uk

Hotel Cipriani & Palazzo Vendramin,
Venice, Italy

However familiar we may be with images — in art, film and literature — of the fragile glory of Venice, it is almost impossible not to be spellbound on arrival by the fading beauty of it all. Add in the romance of a wedding, and you can almost feel the Venetian magic beginning to sweep you off your feet. Dubbed 'La Serenissima' or 'Most Serene' when it was the hub of Renaissance Europe's most powerful merchant empire, this extraordinary city retains that serenity in its ethereal looks — and in its unique status as a city without cars. The Venetian equivalent of a taxi rank is a gondola station, or 'Servizio Gondole', with straw-hatted gondoliers hanging out playing cards and gossiping until their next fare appears, against a backdrop of some of the most impressive architecture in the world.

After touching down at Venice Marco Polo Airport, a five-minute cab ride brings you to the dock, where you board a natty motorboat that speeds off down a watery highway (the driving is every bit as daredevil as its land-based Italian counterpart) leading to a city where Renaissance palaces rise up from green depths and the streets are narrow canals. Arriving by motorboat is de rigueur for Cipriani guests, as the hotel is on the Giudecca, an island in the lagoon. Brown-and-white striped poles like candy sticks mark the posh little dock of the 'Cip', as it is affectionately known, where guests alight to be greeted by charming gentlemen in theatrical capes.

OPPOSITE: AN OPULENT WEDDING RECEPTION IN THE GRANARIES WITH CANDLELIT MURANO GLASS CHANDELIERS.

BELOW: THE CIPRIANI BOASTS THE ONLY SWIMMING POOL IN CENTRAL VENICE.

■ BEST TIME OF YEAR TO GO
May, June and September.

■ CEREMONIES
Couples must wed in the Register Office (Palazzo Cavalli) or a church before heading back to the hotel for a blessing (optional) and reception.

■ PRE-WEDDING RESIDENCY
None required, but it is advisable to allow at least two or three days to make all the final arrangements.

Completed in 1958 by Giuseppe Cipriani, restaurateur extraordinaire and founder of the legendary Harry's Bar, the hotel now exudes an air of knowing luxury: you won't find any designer-led fads here. Giuseppe Cipriani's dream was to build a hotel within easy reach of St Mark's Square, yet far enough away to guarantee peace and privacy. The Giudecca provided just that, and as a consequence has attracted everyone from Orson Welles to Andy Warhol, becoming the chosen residence for many a film star during the Venice Film Festival, including Nicole Kidman.

Couples considering marrying in Venice should get in touch with their local registrar, who will advise them accordingly. The main documents required are a Non-impediment to Marriage certificate, birth certificates and photocopies of passports, which must be sent to the British consulate in Venice together with the consular fee. The British Consulate will liaise with the Italian authorities. Couples need to have their wedding date and the chosen venue confirmed in writing by the Italian Consulate. Wedding blessings and receptions are available at the Cipriani, but couples must marry officially in a civil ceremony, usually at the Palazzo Cavalli near the Rialto Bridge, or have a religious ceremony in a church of their choice. In a Catholic church both religious and civil ceremonies are necessary as in Italy no religious ceremonies alone have legal status. Alternatively, civil ceremonies can also be held in a historic palace or a garden, or even on a gondola. Most couples having their reception at the Cipriani head to the Palazzo Cavalli, Venice's city-centre Register Office. But rest assured as with everything in Venice, there is nothing ordinary about this municipal building. Inside this three-storey 16th-century Renaissance gem is a series of rooms set aside for the bride and groom, including one with 18th-century stucco decoration and a breathtaking panorama over the Grand Canal and the Rialto Bridge. Hanging on the wall is an impressive painting entitled The Golden Wedding, painted in 1909 by the famous Venetian artist Luigi Nono. Couples can arrive at this romantic palazzo — which takes its name from the Cavalli family who lived there, and was later the residence of the American novelist James Fenimore Cooper — by decorated gondola or Cipriani boat. As weddings here are in such demand, it is advisable to book at least a year in advance.

After the legal wedding ceremony, the newlyweds take a boat back to the Cipriani, where there is a choice of venues for a wedding blessing. The Antique Garden (Giardino Antico) can accommodate up to 200 people on lawns right by the waterside, with views of the islands of San Giorgio Maggiore, Santa Maria delle Grazie, San Servolo and San Lazzaro. It also looks towards the Lido and out to the Adriatic Sea. The pretty terrace of the Fortuny Restaurant is available for smaller wedding parties, but it is the fragrant and colourful Casanova Gardens to the rear of the hotel that are the most popular venue. Reputedly a spot where Giacomo Casanova conducted numerous clandestine trysts in the 1750s, this historic garden is filled with romance. It makes a wonderful setting for wedding blessings and receptions, with pretty marquees available.

ABOVE TOP: NATTY MOTORBOATS
ARE ADORNED WITH LILIES FOR
THE WEDDING COUPLE.

ABOVE: CELEBRATING THE START OF
MARRIED LIFE IN ST MARK'S SQUARE.

LEFT: A PRETTY ARBOUR OF VINES IN
THE CIPRIANI GARDENS.

RIGHT: A PALATIAL ROOM IN THE 15TH
CENTURY PALAZZO VENDRAMIN WITH
VIEWS OF ST MARK'S SQUARE.

Near by is the hotel's Vin Salso vineyard (so-named because of the lagoon's salty effect on the grapes). The Cipriani's own wine, Salso de Casanova, is often chosen for weddings. The heights of extravagance are possible here: in recent years a film director had a chapel specially constructed in the gardens, reached by a passageway strewn with rose petals flown in from California.

On the Giudecca Canal itself, opposite St Mark's Square, stands I Granai della Repubblica, or the Granaries of the Venetian Republic. This immense and lofty edifice, with an imposing wooden ceiling, stone floor and exposed brickwork, dates back 500 years, and began life as the granary and storerooms of the Republic of Venice. Air-conditioned or heated, with a sophisticated lighting rig, it is now up and running for 21st-century receptions. A recent wedding celebration here for 450 was a spectacular affair, with candlelit Murano glass chandeliers. Guests can spill out into Cip's Club Restaurant with its water terrace pontoon on the Giudecca Canal and

wraparound views of Venice: this has to be the best dining view in town. Wedding parties can have cocktails on the terrace before heading into the Granaries: bellinis are the order of the day, a refreshing aperitif of fresh peach juice and Champagne.

The original hotel now contains 104 guest rooms, so there is plenty of space for family and friends to spread out. All rooms enjoy superb views of the lagoon to the south, the church and monastery of Palladio's San Giorgio Maggiore to the east, or the walled gardens and vineyards of Casanova to the west. Honeymooners may want to opt for the de luxe apartment in the romantic Palazzo Vendramin, linked to the hotel by an ancient courtyard and flowered loggia. Altogether more romantic, this is a converted 15th-century residence and perhaps qualifies as Venice's first six-star rooms with prices to match. The decor was designed by the late Gerard Gallet in a Venetian style reminiscent of Fortuny, making full use of the high ceilings and carved windows.

Butler service ensures you are waited on hand and foot, and breakfast is prepared in the suite every day. Most breathtaking of all, however, is the view over the lagoon to St Mark's Square and the Doge's Palace. The newly opened Dogaressa Suite is decorated with original Coromandel screens, antique Chinese lamps, and Fortuny and Rubelli fabrics. The suite offers the largest sitting room in the Palazzo, a dreamy bedroom, a pink marble bathroom and splendid views over St Mark's. The Palladio Suite has a 180-degree view over the lagoon through floor-to-ceiling windows in the bedrooms, living room (which can be transformed into a cinema at the touch of a button) and dining area. Newlyweds here have the use of a secluded private garden, a wooden terrace shaded by shrubs and lemon trees and an outdoor Jacuzzi. A further addition to the hotel is the Palazzetto, with five de luxe suites overlooking the basin of San Marco.

The Cipriani boasts the only tennis courts and swimming pool in central Venice — and what a pool, Olympic in proportions and thoroughly chic. The Casanova Spa opened in 2004 overlooking the Casanova Gardens. This top-quality spa has three treatment rooms with decorous Venetian glass lights. The pièce de résistance is the Sea Creation Room, guaranteed to soothe any future bride's or groom's pre-wedding nerves: as they lie back, couples are lulled by waves lapping the walls, sand under glass on the floor and star lights on the ceiling. Treatments and massages range from floating and energizing sessions, perfect for stressed brides-to-be, cranial and Swedish massages, and the restorative technique known as ScenTao, a famed toning and stress-reducing massage using hot stones. Brides-to-be who have had one too many ice creams to fit into their wedding dress might like to try the slimming Proellixe Vibration machine.

A 'Venetian Interlude' package, recommended for honeymooners, includes three nights in a junior suite with Champagne breakfasts, lunch or dinner at any of the Cipriani's restaurants and one special massage or facial treatment in the Casanova Spa. Now that the Venice Opera House has reopened after a seven-year restoration following a fire, newlyweds can take advantage of the Cipriani's 'Opera Package', with their own box reserved for them. Alternatively, marina berths are available if you feel like heading off by private yacht.

As Venice lies at the top of the Adriatic Sea, newlyweds can cruise the east coast of Italy exploring gems like Rimini, or even head to the wonderful coastline of Croatia, dotted with thousands of beautiful islands, nowadays deemed one of the most fashionable cruising destinations in the world.

CIPRIANI'S WATER TERRACE RESTAURANT
ON THE GIUDECCA CANAL.

For more information
Hotel Cipriani & Palazzo Vendramin
Giudecca 10
30133 Venice, Italy
T: +39 041 5207744
E: info@hotelcipriani.it   www.hotelcipriani.com

Italian Tourist Board: www.italiantouristboard.co.uk

The Venice Wedding Planner:
www.theveniceweddingplanner.com

Pangkor Laut Resort, Malaysia

Pangkor Laut Resort is a jewel of a private island retreat. Set off the western coast of the Malaysian peninsula, close to the larger island of Pulau Pangkor and facing the Straits of Malacca, it is a true wedding escape. The island consists of 300 hectares (nearly 750 acres) of two-million-year-old rainforest, only a fifth of which has been developed, so wedding couples here have the feeling that they have discovered their very own romantic jungle hideaway. Pangkor Laut was officially opened in 1991 by Luciano Pavarotti, who fell in love with the place, declaring: 'I almost cried when I saw how beautiful God had made this paradise.'

Couples are met at Pangkor Airport by a hotel representative and whisked off for the three-hour drive to the ferry point at Lumut. Arriving by boat, couples have a panoramic view of Royal Bay, the main part of the resort comprising luxury stilted villas linked by wooden walkways, with the dense jungle rising behind and more villas hidden among the vegetation. Inside, the villas are a blend of Malay and Balinese architecture, with carved wood and rattan furniture. Guests arrive to find the luxurious open-air bath strewn with petals, and a bottle of chilled Champagne awaiting them.

OPPOSITE: A FRANGIPANI FILLED POOL AT THE ULTRA ROMANTIC PANGKOR LAUT RESORT.

BELOW: THE PRIVATE ISLAND OF PANGKOR LAUT TAKES THE BREATH AWAY OF MANY A VISITOR.

■ BEST TIME OF YEAR TO GO
June and July are recommended as the best months, though the climate is tropical and temperatures year-round range from 21 to 32°C (70 to 90°F) with occasional showers.

■ CEREMONIES
Religious (Catholic, Methodist or Anglican) or civil.

■ PRE-WEDDING RESIDENCY
Couples must be resident for a minimum of seven days, including the day of arrival. If they apply for a special licence, the residency requirement is waived.

LEFT: RED CARPET WEDDING VOWS ON THE BEACH AT EMERALD BAY.

RIGHT: PRETTY RECEPTIONS ARE HELD AT 'DINNER ON THE ROCKS'.

OPPOSITE: AN ESPECIALLY MEMORABLE SUNSET AT EMERALD BAY.

Most overseas couples arriving here have left family and friends behind and are in search of an intimate wedding, but Pangkor Laut can cater for wedding parties of up to 120 people. Religious weddings — Catholic, Methodist and Anglican services are available and others can be arranged — are conducted by a priest or pastor, while at civil weddings a registrar officiates. Couples must produce their birth certificates and passports, along with four passport-sized photographs of each of them, taken separately. Also required is a letter from their parish priest or a sworn affidavit confirming that they are free to wed. This must be stamped by the Foreign and Commonwealth Office's Legalization Office. If either party is divorced, a decree absolute must be provided, or a death certificate and previous marriage certificate if they are widowed. Couples must be resident for a minimum of seven days, including the day

of arrival, unless they apply for a special licence to marry, in which case the residency requirement is waived. In this case, staff at Pangkor Laut escort couples to the State Secretary's Office in Ipoh, where the special licence is issued for RM100 (approx £15). Ipoh lies inland on the Malay peninsula and — with its well-preserved old town and some of the best Chinese restaurants in Malaysia — is well worth a visit. If the State Secretary is satisfied with the statutory declaration and the declaration of no lawful impediment, he will grant a licence for marriage, which must take place within a month.

Couples can make their vows on the beach at Emerald Bay, which takes its name from the crystal clear waters of the Straits of Malacca set against a backdrop of the dense jungle. Some 120 guests can be accommodated on the sand, depending on the tide, or it can make an intimate setting for the couple alone. A gazebo is erected on the beach and decorated with floral garlands, and a red carpet can be laid on the sand while a string quartet serenades the union. Ceremonies for up to 30 people can also be held at 'Dinner on the Rocks', a rocky outcrop overlooking Emerald Bay with the jungle behind. This decked area is decorated for the occasion with pretty white flowers in little silver bowls and white ribbons in ornamental branches, which flutter in the sea breezes.

Couples can also tie the knot on board the YTL Lady, a 64-foot luxury yacht decorated with floral garlands, which cruises into the Straits of Malacca for the wedding ceremony. Afterwards, the yacht anchors at Emerald Bay, where up to 18 guests are ferried to the beach while the resident trio serenades the couple. Guests are welcomed ashore with a tropical drink, and dramatic sunsets at Emerald Bay provide the perfect opportunity for wedding photographs. The day ends with a romantic meal at Dinner on the Rocks. If couples wish to add a Malay touch to their wedding, they can hire traditional wedding outfits.

Receptions in the gardens can accommodate a maximum of 120 guests, or up to 30 at Dinner on the Rocks. Wonderful Malay dishes served in clay pots include soto ayam, or chicken soup with local spices, followed by a selection of main dishes such as ikan masak kicap, or fish with spices in soy sauce, and a ketayap dessert — a Malaysian crêpe with a sweetened coconut filling.

Altogether there are 156 rooms and suites, located at Royal Bay, Marina Bay and the Spa Village. Couples can choose to stay in a variety of locations including Royal Hill where the rooms are perched on the hillside among lush vegetation with sweeping sea views, Royal Garden where rooms are scattered about the hillside amid tropical gardens, or Royal Beach with just eight rooms clustered around tropical gardens and only steps away from the sandy beach. However, most dramatic of all is Royal Sea; 21 rooms as well as the luxurious Suria and Purnama Suites are set on stilts over the

emerald-green sea. These stilted rooms are particularly romantic at night when lanterns light the walkways and the sound of the sea can be heard lapping beneath you.

Small family weddings can be accommodated in the Pangkor Laut Estates, on the island's northern coast. Set around a sandy white bay and two encircling promontories, this is a group of eight stunning self-contained properties. Three estates are set on the beach, with the remaining five among the trees on both promontories. Each 'Estate' consists of several pavilions set within a tropical garden, evoking the traditional Malaysian way of life, inextricably linked with its natural surroundings. They range from two to four bedrooms and each has its own chef and personal butler. A personal trainer is even available for those wishing to get in shape before their big day. For healthy-living couples who have come for a truly pampering wedding and

honeymoon, the Spa Village has 22 rooms next to eight treatment rooms, healing huts, a Chinese herbal shop, Ayurvedic and Malay huts, a Wrap House, yoga pavilion, private beach, spa restaurant and boutique. During their stay, couples simply must experience the Belian Treatment Pavilion with its outdoor whirlpool, yoga pavilion, nap gazebo, steam room and private treatment area. The Spa Village offers a variety of treatments for pre-wedding preparations, including manicures, pedicures, hair styling and facials. For more intimate pampering, luxury in-room baths are ideal for wedding couples. This sensuous milk bath is scented with fresh rose petals, kaffir lime and essential oils.

Pangkor Laut offers plenty of opportunities for romantic activities and excursions. Couples can accompany the resort's resident naturalist, Mr Yip Yoon Wah, on his daily trek through the rainforest, where they may

see wildlife ranging from crab-eating macaques to tropical monitor lizards and yellow pied hornbills. Or they can take the 'Pulau Sembilan' or 'Nine Islands' day tour on board a teakwood Chinese tongkang, or junk, to a sequence of nine islands. During the day the vessel anchors in a sheltered cove for snorkelling or lazing on the empty beach, and a sumptuous Indian curry is served on banana leaves. Alternatively, newlyweds may like to charter one of the resort's two luxury yachts to take them wherever they desire. At the resort, meanwhile, windsurfing, sailing, water-skiing and scuba diving are available.

Pangkor Laut offers a 'Romantic Interlude' package, where couples are presented with mementoes including a locally made batik sarong and pareo and a coffee table book about the region's wildlife. They can also take part in a tree-planting ceremony in the rainforest to symbolize their marriage, commemorated by an engraved plaque. In this primordial jungle dating back two million years, what could be a more potent symbol of the longevity of love and marriage?

A DOUBLE TREATMENT PAVILION AT
THE SPA VILLAGE.

For more information
Pangkor Laut Resort
Pangkor Laut Island
32200 Lumut Perak
Malaysia
T: +800 9899 9999
E: travelcentre@ytlhotels.com.my
www.pangkorlaut.com

Tourism Malaysia: www.malaysiatrulyasia.co.uk

Voile d'Or Resort and Spa, Mauritius

Long celebrated as a place of enchantment for visitors, Mauritius famously inspired the American writer Mark Twain to observe: 'You gather the idea that Mauritius was made first and then heaven, and that heaven was copied after Mauritius.' This glorious island, lost in the Indian Ocean just north of the Tropic of Capricorn and more than 1,600 km (1,000 miles) off the coast of southeast Africa, is also now an oasis of pure glamour, with glitzy five-star hotels, fine gourmet restaurants under the auspices of celebrity chefs, sensational spas, elite golf courses and diamond boutiques. Celebrities from Prince William to Victoria Beckham have helped to make it a place to see and be seen, but behind the glitz there remains a magnificent island of largely unspoilt white-sand beaches, the world's longest unbroken coral reef, moody mountains, ylang ylang distilleries, botanical gardens and national parks where stags and wild kestrels thrive. Add to all this a fabulous wealth of different cultural influences, and you have a heady, magical mix that is proving irresistible to ever-increasing numbers of couples wishing to tie the knot.

Throughout the island future brides and grooms are welcomed as VIPs, as are their families and friends. The top resorts effortlessly lay on petal-strewn baths for two, double spa treatments and feet-in-the-sand dinners on moonlit beaches.

OPPOSITE: VOILE D'OR'S WEDDING PAVILION APPEARS TO FLOAT ON A LARGE LILY POND.

BELOW: THE CREATIVE MIND BEHIND VOILE D'OR KNOWS HOW TO DO HOTEL AS THEATRE.

■ BEST TIME OF YEAR TO GO
Mauritius has a subtropical climate, making it a year-round destination. While the winter months from May to October are wonderfully warm and dry, however, the summer months from November to April can be just too hot. This is also the cyclone season, with unpredictable rainy spells.

■ CEREMONIES
Civil or religious.

■ PRE-WEDDING RESIDENCY
For a civil wedding, 24 hours; for a religious ceremony, 15 days.

For a civil wedding, couples must be resident in Mauritius for 24 hours before the ceremony and must sign an affidavit at the Register Office to confirm that they are both free to marry. If a religious ceremony is required, couples must be resident for 15 days before the ceremony. In either case, both bride and groom must bring their original birth certificates and valid 10-year passports. Divorcees need to produce a decree absolute. If the bride has been divorced for less than 10 months, a pregnancy test is mandatory. If either has been widowed, the former spouse's death certificate and the previous marriage certificate must be produced. For religious weddings, couples are also required to produce christening certificates and a certificate of 'good morality' from their respective parish priests, specifying that both are free to marry and are not divorced. Catholics wishing to marry in Mauritius should contact the Port-Louis Diocese for the necessary information.

In the case of civil ceremonies, couples must send photocopies of their documents to The Registry, Civil Status Division E, Anquetil Building, Sir S Ramgoolam Street, Port Louis, Mauritius (tel: +230 2011727). Couples must take all their original documents with them for submission on the wedding day. For a religious wedding, original documents are required six weeks before (or eight weeks if couples are of different religions, as the case must go to their local bishop). Once couples arrive in Mauritius, they must go to the main Registrar's Office in Port Louis to sign an affidavit to confirm that they are both free to marry, which takes about half a day. They also have to go to the Civil Status

Office of the hotel locality to arrange publication of the banns and meet with the Civil Status Officer, who will come to celebrate the ceremony at the hotel. Civil, Seventh-Day Adventist and Hindu weddings can be arranged here, and Voile d'Or's dedicated wedding coordinators promise that there will be only one wedding each day. Booking well ahead is therefore essential to ensure a particular date.

Voile d'Or Resort & Spa is one of a batch of new hotels that opened towards the end of 2004 on the southwest coast of the island, on a 500-m (1,640 ft) stretch of beach at Bel Ombre, among casuarina trees and undulating sand dunes. Philippe Requin, the creative genius behind the resort, knows how to do hotel as theatre: Voile d'Or is huge and visually stunning. Everything from the giant atrium of the reception area to the magnificent fish-filled pond by the cavernous restaurant is larger than life, and just perfect for spectacular weddings. This is heaven for couples who are weary of pared-down boutique chic and want some full-on, old-style glamour. All bells and whistles, it has four swimming pools, four bars and three restaurants, one of which is Le Gavroche des Tropiques, under master chef Michel Roux Jnr, chef patron of the legendary Michelin-starred Le Gavroche in London. Special attractions include the quirkily named Bis'Kit Pottery Workshop and Kiln, where guests can make their own mementoes, and Whiff! Atelier du Parfum, where brides-to-be can blend their unique perfume, future orders of which can be dispatched as required.

ABOVE LEFT: HUGE ROUND BEDS ARE A FEATURE IN MANY OF THE BEDROOMS.

ABOVE RIGHT: NEWLYWEDS RETURN TO THEIR ROOM TO FIND CHAMPAGNE AND A FLOWER FILLED BATH.

OPPOSITE: A GRACEFUL WEDDING FOR TWO AT VOILE D'OR.

Weddings take place everywhere from shady coves and gazebos floating among water lilies, to historic colonial mansions. Nothing, it seems, is too much trouble here. Large wedding parties from overseas are not unusual in Mauritius, and are well catered for.

The resort's wedding gazebo is one of the most impressive on the island. Apparently floating in the middle of a giant lily pond, and reached only by a row of stepping stones, it makes a wonderous location for a ceremony and photographs, as it overlooks the resort's white-sand beach and the ocean.

Other wedding locations here include the spectacular lobby, the roof of Sirocco Beach Bistro and Bar, the garden in front of the luxurious Royal Suite with its private pool, the beach or the jetty, or even on board a catamaran. Whatever the venue, it can be decorated with tropical flowers such as the ubiquitous but exotic red and pink anthuriums and swathes of silk.

If couples wish to add a specifically Mauritian touch, the brides can wear a colourful sega dancer's dress, or for a Hindu-style wedding saris are available.

Brides can be escorted from their room to the wedding venue by a local sega group with a guitarist playing the wedding march, or arrive by boat.

Receptions can be arranged around the hotel, depending on the size of the wedding party. For intimate celebrations, a wedding gazebo can be laid out for a romantic candlelit dinner for between two and eight people. Those with more guests attending can head to Le Gavroche des Tropiques, the Royal Suite or the roof of Sirocco. Alternatively, just behind the Poussada Restaurant is Le Cirné, a private dining room seating up to 14. Large parties can dine on the beach at Sirocco, with a bonfire and private sega show. There is no shortage of musical talent in Mauritius, so any entertainment from a jazz trio to a torch-song crooner can accompany the celebrations. The dark and exotic Shahrazad, the resort's Arabian Nights-inspired nightclub, is a great place for the wedding party to dance the night away, or snuggle up in a velvet-lined alcove to sip cocktails and smoke one of the hookah pipes on offer.

There are 181 rooms to choose from at Voile d'Or, all of which are an impressive size and have round double bathtubs and large balconies with an ocean view. Wedding couples are bound to fall for the charms of Room 1117, with its huge tub on a private outdoor terrace, four-poster bed and lounge with a bar, or the romance of Room 1025, which has a huge round bed with pink roses and curtains that can be drawn around it. Newlyweds return to their rooms to find Champagne and beautiful flower arrangements awaiting them.

Pre- and post-wedding spa treatments for couples are offered at the Spa Aldana. A Yasmin & Simbad is a half-day pampering for couples, including a complete body massage, a milk bath with a loving cup of Champagne, and a rubdown of sensuous Aldana Body Milk. The treatment rooms are semi-submerged, giving a sense of tranquillity and peace. The beautifully designed hammam, meanwhile, is in Turkish style, with steam rooms and cold plunge pools to detox and stimulate the body.

There is plenty to entertain everybody after the big day. Stunning golf courses include one designed by Bernard Langer on its very own tropical island at Ile aux Cerfs. Watersports range from scuba diving to windsurfing, or deep-sea fishing is an exhilarating option, as the coast is home to marlin sharks, tuna and barracuda. Shopaholics, meanwhile, may like to explore Port Louis's Caudan Waterfront and market or Grand Baie's shopping boulevards. Voile d'Or is the place to go for a full-on glamour wedding in the sun, or as Mark Twain might have put it, a match made in heaven.

AN INTIMATE WEDDING RECEPTION DINNER.

For more information
Voile d'Or Resort and Spa
Bel Ombre, Mauritius
T: +230 466 1900
E: info@voiledor.com
www.voiledor.com

Mauritius Tourism Promotion Board:
www.mauritiustourism.co.uk
Port-Louis Diocese (for Catholic weddings):
T: +230 208 3068

One&Only Palmilla,
Los Cabos, Mexico

The sheer drama of Mexico's Baja California Peninsula with its crashing turquoise surf and spectacular beaches is enough to make any newlyweds swoon. Add to that the grace and luxury of the One&Only Palmilla with its traditional Mexican chapel on the hill, red-tiled roofs, whitewashed walls, fountains and swaying palms, and it soon becomes apparent why more and more couples are heading there to tie the knot. The area is infused with romance as this is where the ocean greets the mountainous desert and the Pacific merges with the Sea of Cortez. It's not unusual to catch sight of grey whales rising beyond the surf as you celebrate your wedding vows.

From the moment couples arrive at One&Only Palmilla, by a private chauffeured Hummer H2, the pampering begins. Faces are given a refreshing Evian water mist spray and chilled towels are offered. By the time couples have been introduced to their personal 24-hour butler, they begin to get the reassuring feeling that their nuptial stay will be something special.

OPPOSITE: A FEET IN THE SAND RECEPTION ON THE SPECTACULAR BEACH AT ONE&ONLY PALMILLA.

BELOW: THE RESORT'S TRADITIONAL MEXICAN CHAPEL HAS A MAJESTIC SETTING OVERLOOKING THE RESORT.

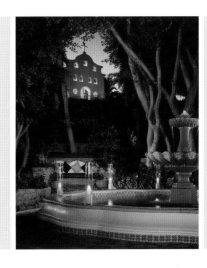

■ **BEST TIME OF YEAR TO GO**
April, May and October.

■ **CEREMONIES**
In Mexico only civil marriages are recognized as legal. Couples may have a religious ceremony but it will have no legal validity. A blessing after the legal civil ceremony is recommended.

■ **PRE-WEDDING RESIDENCY**
No Mexican residential requirements apply, but you should allow a few days for legal checks.

Blood tests are required in Los Cabos two working days before the wedding, in accordance with Mexican law. Couples who have been married before must prove that a year has elapsed since their divorce or the death of their previous spouse. There must be a minimum of four witnesses, but the hotel is happy to provide these if necessary.

Couples may opt to tie the knot against the stunning backdrop of the beach or on the Cantamar Terrace, in a ceremony conducted in Spanish by a Justice of the Peace from Los Cabos. Translators are available if requested in advance. But perhaps One&Only Palmilla's greatest attraction for weddings is its chapel, built in 1956 along with the original resort. Perched on a hill overlooking tropical grounds with the ocean beyond, it is in traditional Mexican style with a towering white façade.

The most atmospheric option by far is a chapel wedding with up to 50 guests. The new One&Only Spa near by offers a special VIP salon where wedding parties can prepare for the festivities, and a horse-drawn carriage with footman is on hand to transport the couple to the chapel and reception. For the ceremony, a magical scene is created when the chapel's 16 windows are candlelit, and the altar is adorned with a white cloth, candelabras and tropical blooms, ensuring a very special feel to the occasion.

Nuptials on the beach are also popular, given the dramatic coastline with its crashing surf and turquoise waters. Brass tiki torches in the sand mark out a private

ABOVE: THE ENCHANTING ENTRANCE TO ONE&ONLY PALMILLA SETS THE MEXICAN TONE.

OPPOSITE: THE CHAPEL WAS BUILT IN 1956 ALONG WITH THE REST OF THE RESORT AND SEATS 50.

One&Only is a hotel group that is pushing the boundaries of the five-star tag and their Mexican resort is no exception. Its unusual and highly romantic touches include swinging beds by the ocean and telescopes in rooms to stargaze. Once the tropical hideaway of the likes of writer Ernest Hemingway and Hollywood actress Jean Harlow, One&Only Palmilla was founded in 1956 by Don Abelardo Rodriguez, son of General Abelardo Rodriguez, the interim president of Mexico. It has recently been restored to its now-legendary Mexican splendour following a $90 million refurbishment completed in February 2004. Set on one of the few swimming beaches in the region, the resort encompasses 1 square km (250 acres) of a 3.6 sq km (900 acre) site that includes private residences and a 27-hole golf course designed by Jack Nicklaus.

and very romantic area containing a table draped with white linen and a choopah or an arch of flowers, with white wooden chairs for the guests. Alternatively, the Cantamar Terrace is located at the edge of a grassy area overlooking the ocean. Here the set-up is similar to a beach wedding, with a table covered with white linen and atmospheric torches. One of the resort's most spectacular weddings was a ceremony for 40 on the beach, where the resort's staff constructed a platform over the shallow part of the sea. Here the guests had dinner, creating the heavenly impression that the entire party was floating in the middle of the Sea of Cortez.

Wedding receptions can also be held on the beach by candlelight, or in the C Restaurant, designed by the legendary Charlie Trotter

whose Chicago establishment is considered among the best in America. Private dining rooms can be reserved. Alternatively, the palapa-style Agua Restaurant offers gourmet Mexiterranean cuisine and panoramic views of the infinity-edge pool and the Sea of Cortez. Its fountain courtyard, festive tile decoration and windows open to the tropical breeze create a wonderful atmosphere. In the evening local musicians serenade the newlyweds. A choice of 12 wedding cakes ranges from white chocolate Grand Marnier to guava pineapple.

Rooms and suites are spaciously arranged in single- and three-storey buildings or 'casas' encircling the resort's grounds along the edge of the peninsula, all with a patio or balcony overlooking the sea.

There is personal butler service and fresh fruit of your choice delivered daily. The de luxe one-bedroom suites in Casa Mananitas enjoy magnificent views of the sun rising over the Sea of Cortez and feature hand-crafted Mexican woodwork and decorative art. Private terraces have a daybed where couples can lie back and enjoy the tropical views.

The new One&Only Spa at Palmilla takes its inspiration from the architectural and artistic heritage of Mexico. Thirteen private treatment villas easily accommodate two and have air-conditioned massage pavilions opening on to a tropical garden. Couples can enjoy a 'Pathway to Love Spa Couples Ritual' in a private villa, including a personal yoga class, an ultimate spa ritual for two involving a wellbeing massage, and an exotic flower bath with a waterfall shower. Hydrotherapy facilities include steam and sauna rooms as well as a watsu (water shiatsu) pool. For a wedding infused with local culture and the most amazing setting, One&Only Palmilla is hard to beat. If it warmed the romantic heart of writer Ernest Hemingway, it's sure to inspire today's wedding couples.

For more information
One&Only Palmilla
Los Cabos
Mexico
T: +52 624 146 7000
E: reservations@oneandonlypalmilla.com,
www.oneandonlypalmilla.com

Mexico Tourism Board:
www.visitmexico.com

Prestonfield,

The romance of Scotland pervades its capital city in every cobbled street and each gleaming façade. Any city that can create a festival of the arts as vibrant as the Fringe has proved its romantic spirit. Edinburgh is a city that has retained its heart and soul while embracing the new cool of designer bars, shops and boutiques. Brides-to-be in search of the perfect dress can choose between old-school Jenners or designer-led Harvey Nichols. Couples arriving by train emerge from Waverley Station to the vista of Princes Street Gardens and the castle beyond, sitting grandly on its rocky perch. Successfully marrying something old with something new, Edinburgh has an elegance about it that makes it a top wedding destination.

For a traditional Scottish wedding with a healthy dose of Gothic Revival extravagance and a wickedly camp sense of spectacle, Prestonfield is a gem. The society magazine *Tatler* described a stay at this sexy hotel as akin to 'living in one of Vivienne Westwood's dresses'. Set in 8 hectares (20 acres) of photogenic parklands, complete with majestic Highland cattle and the odd peacock, this A-listed baroque mansion built for a former Lord Provost of Edinburgh in 1687 is tucked neatly beside Arthur's Seat and the Palace of Holyroodhouse (the present Queen's residence when in town). Despite the countrified feeling, it's just 10 minute's drive from Waverley Station and the heart of downtown Edinburgh, and so is ideal for those who like the idea of a Scottish country house hotel wedding while at the same time remaining wedded to city life.

OPPOSITE: THE ITALIAN ROOM HAS PAINTED SCENES FROM AN 18TH-CENTURY ITALIAN GRAND TOUR.

BELOW: THIS A-LISTED BAROQUE MANSION IS NOW A HOMAGE TO DECADENT LIVING.

- ■ **BEST TIME OF YEAR TO GO**
June to September for a summer wedding, December to March for a winter wedding.

- ■ **CEREMONIES**
Civil or religious weddings may be held in the house itself.

- ■ **PRE-WEDDING RESIDENCY**
No residence in Scotland is required.

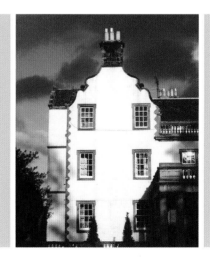

ABOVE: HAVE A TRADITIONAL
SCOTTISH WEDDING OR GO AS
WACKY AS YOU LIKE.

OPPOSITE ABOVE: THERE'S NO
SHORTAGE OF CREATIVE FLAIR
AT PRESTONFIELD.

OPPOSITE BELOW: SPEND YOU FIRST
NIGHT IN A SILVER SLEIGH BED IN
THE FRANKLIN SUITE.

The magic of marrying at Prestonfield is due to the imagination of its owner James Thomson and his team. Together they have recreated an era of ostentatious opulence at Prestonfield, which reopened its doors in 2004. Whether for love's young dream or for *liaisons dangereuses*, this is the place to come. Handsome porters clad in black kilts are on hand to greet couples at the front door and usher them into a world of life-size cherubs on the ceiling, velvet-upholstered walls, damask sofas, dramatic flowers and masses of candles. Here even the ladies' powder room has crystal wall lights, pink drapes and an open fire.

Couples can have a civil wedding with a registrar, or a religious ceremony with a Church of Scotland minister — though one minister was heard to remark that he felt rather out of place at Prestonfield as his blue cassock just wasn't grand enough for the cardinal-red decor. A religious ceremony can take place anywhere, either in or out of doors, but couples should always contact the minister concerned beforehand to make sure he or she is willing to marry couples from outside the parish. Alternatively, a religious ceremony can be held in a nearby church such as Duddingston Kirk, which still has the old family pews of Prestonfield, followed by a reception at the house.

Both parties must submit a Notice of Intention to Marry form along with the fee to the local registrar. These forms are available from the General Register

Office for Scotland between 15 days and three months before the wedding. Formerly, couples used to have to establish residency for a number of days in Scotland — which is why in 1953, when the late James Goldsmith and the heiress Isabel Patino eloped together, they hid out in the attics here while her father searched for them.

Nowadays smaller wedding parties have the choice of booking one of Prestonfield's sumptuous private dining rooms or romantic salons. There is a choice of seven. The Yellow Room, with its 17th-century chinoiserie cabinet — original to the house but sold and later recovered by the current owner — black crocodile sofas and open fire, has an atmosphere of slightly kinky cosiness. The Italian Room boasts the most exquisite panelling and a panorama of painted scenes from an 18th-century Italian Grand Tour. This magical room was the dining room where Johnson and Boswell were entertained, and its star-studded reputation continues today. A candle-lit chandelier and deep red roses make it a beautiful setting for evening ceremonies and receptions.

The Whisky Room, meanwhile, goes to the heart of Scottish culture, with a vast range of malts lining the cabinets and a sofa made from antlers bought at auction in Paris. To the rear of the house is the Garden Room, hung with hand-painted chinoiserie silk wallpaper with a charming bird motif, which many couples pick as their theme for invitations and the like. Part of the beauty of this room lies in its french windows opening out on to the lawns, which makes it a good choice for weddings with children.

Upstairs, the Stuart Room is another exquisitely panelled private dining room. Rich, ripe and dissolute, with a dramatic red, black and gold decor and spectacular baronial thrones, this is a truly sumptuous room where guests will feel very regal. The baroque 17th-century Tapestry Room, with its vast stone fireplace, bacchanalian plaster ceiling and ancient Mortlake tapestries, is normally a public space, but if the wedding party has exclusive use of the house it can be used for wedding ceremonies. A small rooftop patio over the entrance to the house is fantastic for reception drinks on a warm summer's evening. Perhaps the sexiest room in which to wed, however, is the Leather Room, so-called because it is clad entirely in its original 17th-century gilded Cordoba leather wallpaper. It holds just six guests.

At the other end of the scale, a marquee for up to 1200 guests can be erected in the grounds for the wedding ceremony and reception. Marquees with clear roofs are the most popular, as they give guests gorgeous views of Arthur's Seat and the surrounding parkland. The historic converted stables, a huge rotunda of a building in the grounds, can seat between 120 and 500 guests for a wedding reception. A private dinner for the MTV Awards' entire cast was held here, with guests including Beyoncé, Kylie Minogue and Justin Timberlake. The red walls are decorated with mirrors and twinkling starlights, and a professional lighting rig guarantees a dramatic effect. But of course a traditional Scottish ceilidh wedding is what Prestonfield does best. If the weather is fine, guests can have drinks on the lawn before the bride and groom are piped into the rotunda. For winter or evening receptions, flaming torches light their way.

For totally private weddings, couples can hire the entire hotel for 24 or 48 hours, with all its 22 rooms and two suites. Otherwise there are plenty of good B&Bs near by in Newington, or you could always send more affluent guests to Prestonfield's sister hotel, The Witchery by the Castle. Prestonfield's Rhubarb Restaurant, can seat up to 50 guests but is available for wedding receptions only with exclusive use of the whole house. The head chef strives to deliver the finest banqueting in Scotland, to ecstatic reviews. The choice of six wedding menus, named after magazines, moves up the scale from 'Cosmo' to 'Vogue'. 'Vogue' is a magnificent five-course feast, starting with marinated lobster with crab and avocado salsa and finishing with a dark chocolate and mascarpone tart and lavish cheeseboard. The resident sommelier will help you choose the perfect wines for your celebration.

As for wedding themes and decorations, James Thomson and his team are renowned for pushing the boat out. One couple liked the hotel's scarlet ostrich-feathered Christmas trees so much that they requested a recreation of them in a white winter wonderland wedding, with thousands of white ostrich feathers – amazingly, it also snowed on the day – a feat the team like to pretend they prearranged! For a bride and groom who were dairy farmers, Prestonfield had ice cream made from their herds and the newlyweds left on a decorated milk float. Others have departed in a hot-air balloon. For a spot of true star treatment, the happy couple may arrive or depart by helicopter, as Prestonfield is the only hotel in Edinburgh with its own helipad.

A wedding night at Prestonfield is – naturally – another grand affair. Rooms are an opulent swathe of reds and blacks, with padded brocade walls, antique chairs as big as thrones, gilt-framed mirrors and quirky details such as oriental birdcages. Hidden behind the swagger, meanwhile, is state-of-the-art technology including plasma-screen television, Bose sound systems and air conditioning. The beds are sumptuous, with sybaritic velvet throws, and couples will always find a bottle of Pol Roger Champagne awaiting them, along with a delicacy such as a duo of chocolate mousse served in shot glasses. If the rooms seem the ultimate in glamorous opulence, there are also two grand suites on the first floor of the main house. The Ramsay Suite, named after Allan Ramsay, the celebrated 18th-century portrait painter, reflects the grandeur of Edinburgh Old Town, with its huge couch and original tapestry upholstery. But it is the Franklin Suite, so-named because Benjamin Franklin visited Prestonfield, that is generally regarded as the one for newlyweds, with its clean lines evoking the Regency style of Edinburgh's New Town and, more romantically, an enormous sleigh bed finished in silver leaf.

The overall opulent setting of Prestonfield makes an impressive venue for a wedding. With the help of Prestonfield's efficient team of wedding coordinators and events stylists, couples are sure to have a day to remember with every possible detail taken care of, from the flickering candles to casually strewn rose petals, artfully beribboned napkins and fabulous flowers.

ABOVE: LIFE SIZED CHERUBS ON THE CEILING ARE THE NORM.

OPPOSITE: GOTHIC REVIVAL EXTRAVAGANCE AT PRESTONFIELD.

For more information
Prestonfield House, Prestonfield Road, Edinburgh, Scotland EH16 5UT
T: +44 (0)131 225 7800
E: weddings@prestonfield.com   www.prestonfield.com

Duddingston Kirk: www.itido.com
Register Office for Scotland: www.gro-scotland.gov.uk
Scottish Tourist Board: www.visitscotland.com

Frégate Island Private, Seychelles

Biblically speaking, the Seychelles is the original place for love. This stunning archipelago of 115 tropical islands, scattered over a million square kilometres (nearly 4,000 square miles) in the Indian Ocean, has been claimed as the lost site of the Garden of Eden. There is no denying the fact that these islands are among the most pristine and romantic in the world, with an array of untouched forests, bird sanctuaries, exotic hideaways, virgin fishing grounds and spectacular diving spots.

Frégate Island Private combines this touch of Eden with superstar style. James Bond himself has holidayed here, in the form of Pierce Brosnan, and Brad Pitt and Jennifer Aniston honeymooned here in happier times. Whether couples choose to marry on a deserted beach at sunset, in the quaint thatched island chapel, on the deck of a yacht or on the granite summit of Mount Signal with flower petals drifting down from a hovering helicopter, Frégate promises a magical day.

Arabian sailors were aware of the island's existence as early as the 7th century, but chose not to settle here. In the late 17th century Frégate's isolation and impenetrable vegetation made it a popular haunt for pirates. Ian Fleming, author of the James Bond books, remained convinced that there was still a treasure trove of booty to be discovered here.

OPPOSITE: A TOUCH OF EDEN WITH SUPERSTAR STYLE AT FRÉGATE ISLAND PRIVATE.

BELOW: THIS LUXURY ISLAND RESORT IS ABOUT THE SIZE OF LONDON'S REGENT'S PARK.

■ BEST TIME OF YEAR TO GO
All year round.

■ CEREMONIES
Civil.

■ PRE-WEDDING RESIDENCY
Three days with a special licence, 11 days without.

ABOVE: A WEDDING DINNER FOR TWO WITH CANDLES IN THE SAND.

ABOVE RIGHT: THERE ARE JUST 16 VILLAS ALL WITH ROMANTIC FOUR-POSTER BEDS.

The islands of the Seychelles fall into two distinct groups, the granitic Inner Islands that lie within the relatively shallow Seychelles plateau, 4 degrees south of the Equator, and the low-lying coraline Outer Islands that lie beyond the plateau up to 10 degrees south of the Equator. Frégate Island lies some 55 km (35 miles) east of the main island of Mahé (a 20-minute helicopter ride away), and is the most distant and fertile of the granitic Inner Island group, surrounded by its own coral reef. This island is a unique microcosm measuring some 3 sq km (just over a square mile, or about the size of London's Regent's Park) that is home to no fewer than 50 species of bird, including the rare Seychelles magpie robin, the Seychelles white-eye and the frigate bird, with its huge wingspan of around 2 m (6 ft), from which the island takes its name. The island is also home to numerous giant

tortoises, while hawksbill turtles lay their eggs undisturbed on its sandy beaches. Couples can explore Frégate with the resident ecologist, who will guide them through the cashew thickets and banyan trees, and explain about the 60,000 indigenous trees that have been planted (so far) and other impressive aspects of this eco-friendly paradise. The feeling of naturally dense jungle remains: this is not an island with the odd solitary palm on a beach. Rather, a lush forest of palms cascades all the way down from the island's peaks to its stunning beaches.

At least two months before travelling to the Seychelles, couples must make arrangements for obtaining a marriage licence with the Senior Officer of the Civil Status Office on the main island of Mahé. They must give the dates of the visit, the name of the hotel where the ceremony will take place and a preferred wedding day date with alternatives. Frégate must also confirm that the chosen date is acceptable and advise a suitable time of day. Certified copies of all required legal documents should be sent, and the originals should be brought for the ceremony. The Civil Status Office will confirm the date of the wedding with fee details. Couples must normally be in the Seychelles for 11 days before tying the knot, but they can obtain exemption by applying for a special licence, which is generally issued two days after application. Marriages can be solemnized immediately afterwards. Frégate's own wedding coordinator will happily assist with all the details.

There is no best time of year for weddings here, as the sun shines most of the time, the rain falls predominantly at night, and temperature and humidity remain constant throughout the year. Civil ceremonies are the norm for overseas visitors, and can take place almost anywhere. Seychellois law does not recognize religious ceremonies, so even if couples wish to wed in the island chapel on Frégate this will still be a civil ceremony, though they can have a religious blessing as well. The wedding coordinator on Frégate should be advised in advance of the couple's religious requirements.

Weddings on the beach are sublime. There are seven to choose from but Anse Victorin is revered as one of the most beautiful in the world, with distinctive granite boulders and a wide sweep of caster-sugar white sand. Anse Macquereau, known as the 'honeymoon beach', is reserved for two people only, and

even has its own 'Do Not Disturb' sign and a two-way radio for drinks orders — the perfect retreat for the day after the wedding.

The rustic island chapel, set on lawns by the sea, is modest in style, with a wide thatched roof and whitewashed wooden columns. It is open to the elements, with

INDULGE IN SIDE BY SIDE MASSAGES AT THE ROCK SPA.

great views of the sea so there is no sense of being shut away inside, and for weddings the small altar is decorated with tropical flowers, confetti and candles.

Simple wedding ceremonies can be arranged on Mount Signal – the highest point of the island at 125m (410 ft). From the summit there are breathtaking views of the canopy of green palms and the sea beyond. It makes a romantic and private spot for newlyweds to enjoy the ocean view at sunset with champagne and canapés, with flower petals scattered all around. Ceremonies can also take place on board the Frégate Bird, an impressive 13 m (43 ft) power craft used for touring between the islands.

As for the reception, the island philosophy is that anything is possible, including celebratory dinners by the light of a bonfire under the stars, live music performances on the beach, discos, gala dinners, private beach picnics or romantic candlelit dinners. For couples wanting a local Seychellois feel, a Creole reception at the Old Plantation House can be arranged, with a wedding breakfast featuring Creole dishes such as curry, bouillabaisse (fish soup) and kat-kat (green bananas cooked in sweet coconut milk). Creole dances such as the sega with their African rhythms, and traditional French dances such as the contredanse and kamtole are popular, accompanied by fiddles, banjos and accordion players – all make for a lively celebration in the middle of the Indian Ocean.

Wedding parties should be aware that wine and champagne are particularly expensive in the Seychelles as they have to be imported, so either bring some duty-free or try the local rum-based jungle juice, bakka, or calou, made from coconut milk and best tasted straight from the tree.

Accommodation on the island consists of just 16 villas scattered between the palm trees, offering total privacy, and provides room for a maximum of 32 in a wedding party. Each villa is built of native mahogany, in harmony with its natural surroundings. Two villas lie within their own secluded tropical gardens. The remaining 14 stand on cliffs high above the sea, offering glimpses through the palm fronds of sister islands set in the emerald and turquoise sea. Below you, glistening waves crash on the white coral sand. This is a wonderful place to feel nature bringing all your senses alive, as you live and sleep above the sea.

PALATIAL BATHROOMS OVERLOOK
THE OCEAN.

All the villas have a large entrance foyer, a living room, a bedroom and french windows that can be opened to the constant cooling breeze. The architecture is Indonesian in inspiration, and the bedrooms are decorated with elegant bric-a-brac such as Javanese sculptures and hand-painted South African pottery. Thai silk pillows and carved furniture from Africa and Asia create wonderfully exotic interiors. Four-poster beds are draped with huge mosquito nets, and fresh hibiscus blooms are laid out for honeymooners. The sumptuous bathing facilities include an outdoor shower fringed by bougainvillea, hibiscus and sweet-smelling frangipani, and the heavenly coconut soap sets the senses tingling. Baths are set beside wraparound windows, so couples can lie back and soak up the views. Outside, personal Jacuzzis are set down wooden walkways, beside a king-size daybed under a white canopy. The perfect climate — warm, moist and fresh all at once — combined with the luxurious treatments available at the Rock Spa located on its high plateau, with on-site apothecary and indigenous treatments, guarantees a glowing complexion for brides on their big day.Hair and make-up artists are available on request to pamper the bridal group, ensuring that make-up, hair and floral arrangements blend harmoniously with the chosen theme, whether it is a natural or a sun-kissed beach look.

A 19th-century British governor described the Seychelles as being 'a thousand miles away from the rest of the world': his words still ring true today, and for those in search of a romantic hideaway, what could be more perfect?

For more information
Frégate Island Private, Seychelles
T: 00 248 670 100
E: info@fregate.com
www.fregate.com

Seychelles Tourist Board:
www.aspureasitgets.com
The Civil Status Office in the Seychelles:
T: 00 248 383182

Singita Private Game Reserve, South Africa

The Africa of dawn safaris and fiery sunsets over the savannah is a deeply romantic place: it gets under the skin and won't leave you alone. Singita Private Game Reserve in the Sabi Sand Reserve, adjacent to the Kruger National Park in South Africa, has captured many a heart: one of the most revered game lodges in the world (safari veterans consider it the best), it pulls out all the stops for an intimate and soulful safari wedding.

Kruger and Sabi Sand covers nearly two million hectares and was established in 1898 to protect the wildlife of the South African Lowveld. Nature-loving couples have come to the right place, as here there are impressive numbers of species including 336 trees, 34 amphibians, 114 reptiles, 507 birds and 147 mammals. Man's interaction with the environment is also apparent from the bushman rock paintings to the luxury lodges of today, of which Singita is definitely top of the evolutionary tree.

Ebony Lodge and Boulders Lodge both have room for 18 guests, and friends and family are greeted with open arms, though children under 10 are not allowed unless either lodge is block-booked by the wedding party. Luxuriating in the shade of gnarled knobthorn and jackalberry trees above the Sand River, Ebony Lodge seems to bathe in a cool silence that is both intoxicating to the senses and anathema to stress. Waking up each morning to the sight of the great savannah plain, viewed in all its glory from the privacy of your deck, is simply breathtaking.

OPPOSITE: EBONY LODGE DECKS OVERLOOK THE GREAT SAVANNAH PLAIN.

BELOW: LANTERNS LIGHT YOUR WAY THROUGH KNOBTHORN AND JACKALBERRY TREES.

■ BEST TIME OF YEAR TO GO
All year round.

■ CEREMONIES
Methodist.

■ PRE-WEDDING RESIDENCY
None required.

In the decor of the lodge, beadwork and the rich colours of the African savannah add a vibrant sense of the local culture, mingling with pieces from the colonial era and new ochre furnishings. Boulders Lodge, meanwhile, is a monumental construction of stone, timber and thatch anchored to the rocky geology of the Sand River Valley. The elemental curves and contemporary African style of the suites are highlighted with touches of fresh blues and greens, and the encounter between sophistication and wilderness, between the narrow horizons of everyday life and the awe-inspiring soul of Africa, can leave none of the reserve's visitors untouched – least of all those about to marry.

The African bush has its unique beauty all through the year. Spring and summer (October to April) bring very warm days, with stunning sunsets that are just perfect for romantic dinners under the African sky. Autumn and winter (May to September) bring warm days and crisp evenings, though this merely serves to add to the romance, as couples can take a dip in their heated

A WEDDING RECEPTION UNDER AFRICAN SKIES.

plunge pools and relax with a glass of South Africa's finest Cap Classic around their fireplace. Weddings are held year-round. A Methodist minister conducts the ceremony, and will contact the couple to discuss the relevant documentation well in advance of the big day. As the minister has to make a 300 km (190 mile) round trip from White River, there is a fee of R1,500 (£120) for his services, plus an additional R850 (£70) if couples have a late afternoon ceremony, as he has to stay overnight at the lodge. Once at Singita, the minister requires the temporary residence number that is given to visitors on arrival in South Africa. The ceremony is simple, and a copy of the service can be sent to the couple in advance; changes such as personalized vows and readings may be made only with the minister's consent.

Wedding ceremonies are usually held on the extensive wooden decks beneath the ancient ebony trees. This lovely area overlooks the Sand River, where hippo and crocodile can be heard grunting their territorial calls. The birdsong, and especially the calls of the fish eagle and purple-crested louries, also add a uniquely African background note to the exchanging of vows, while the antics of the lodge's resident vervet monkey often add a touch of humour. The bride walks down the wooden staircase to meet her waiting groom on the lower deck, which can seat up to 50 guests. As she does so, a choir of local women in traditional African dress sing songs of happiness and praise in the local Shangaan language, as well as when the ceremony is over. With their colourful wraps, headdresses and beaded chains, they make an eye-catching addition to the proceedings.

The wedding reception can take any form the couple desires, from an à la carte dinner in a crystal-set dining suite to a lower-deck dinner overlooking the Sand River, with the jackelberry tree lit up with lanterns. Singita's executive chef, Gary Coetzee, has worked in the food capitals of the globe, and combines the best of Western cuisine with the superb flavours of Africa. Alternatively, a boma or bush dinner under the African moon, with the warmth of the boma fire and the singing of the Shangaan choir, makes a more informal and authentically African experience. Wedding dishes can include the traditional bobotie, a Cape Malay dish of gently curried ground beef topped with baked custard. For more adventurous palates, there are esoteric delicacies such as fillet of ostrich with a cinnamon expresso *jus*. In addition, Singita allegedly has the best bush cellar in Africa, buried deep in the cool rock below Boulders with more than 12,000 bottles of South African and international wines. As for the wedding cake, Singita offers a traditional English fruitcake with white icing or a sponge cake.

ABOVE TOP: A BATH WITH A VIEW
AT BOULDERS LODGE.

ABOVE: EBONY LODGE.

So remote is the location that wedding arrangements need to be carefully orchestrated in advance, as fresh flowers need to be transported and the nearest hairdresser is 150 km (95 miles) away. Female staff at the lodge are usually very happy to assist the bride-to-be with a basic hairdo. A photographer should also be booked well ahead: wonderful wedding shots can be taken out in the bush, usually accompanied by sundowner champagne and canapés.

Before and after the ceremony, couples can pamper themselves in the Bush Spa, which takes a holistic approach to indulging both body and mind. Most treatments are available for couples together, either in their suite or out on the spa decks, where they are lulled by the birdsong and the rustling of the wind through the ebony trees. A Body Bliss treatment detoxifies the skin with a crystal rub and Buchu gel pack, while legs are massaged with Cape camomile-infused creams. Any remaining tension is eased away with an African head and back massage. Alternatively, a Big Five Therapy involves two therapists and begins with a cleansing crystal rub and moisturizing body wrap during which you receive a scalp massage and reflexology. Couples can have this treatment in the privacy of their suite, completed by a sensuous milk bath for two. Most brides opt for manicures to show off their wedding ring to its best effect, and here the manicure includes a jojoba bead hand scrub followed by a nourishing clay mask and hand massage. Even the gyms at Boulders and Ebony are spectacular, with their own steam rooms and the chance to enjoy the wide-open spaces of the African bush through floor-to-ceiling glass walls as you work out.

A special honeymoon treat can be arranged one evening, usually after a game drive. Newlyweds arrive back to find their suite lit up with candles, soft African music playing, a hot bubble bath in their Victorian-style tub, surrounded by scattered petals, and Champagne on ice. Soft slippers and cosy dressing gowns are placed near by. A romantic candlelit dinner is served out on their private deck in the moonlight in summer, or around their fireplace in winter. But honeymoons at Singita are also about the safari experience. There are a number of ways to view the wildlife. Couples can take it easy and simply gaze at the game from the viewing decks, with their unparalleled panorama. Alternatively, they can reserve sole use of a Land-Rover to make the experience more intimate, and take a daytime game drive to spot the 'Big Five' – elephant, rhino, leopard, lion and buffalo – so-called not because of their size, but because they are the most dangerous of all African animals to hunt. There are also the 'Little Five' – buffalo weaver, elephant shrew, leopard tortoise, ant lion and rhino beetle. Evening expeditions into the bush, with fiery skies as the backdrop to rare and timid nocturnal creatures, are even more romantic. For the fearless, guided bush walks are also available. Those in search of more honeymoon adventure and luxury can take the short flight up to the sister property, Singita Lebombo, which was named Hotel of the Year in 2004 in the prestigious UK *Tatler* Travel Awards. Situated on an exclusive 15,000 hectare private concession on the remote eastern boundary of the Kruger National Park, it has the highest concentration of wildlife in the entire park. The lodge itself is an architectural, design and conservation feat at the cutting edge of eco-tourism and is constructed almost entirely of bleached wood and glass.

It's no coincidence that Singita means 'the miracle' in the local language. Couples choosing to tie the knot here are sure to feel the warmth of the Africa spirit. To add to their strong memories and those all-important wedding photographs, couples can visit the Singita boutique to buy each other a keepsake, such as a solid silver cuff in imitation of crocodile skin. A little bit of Africa to take home as man and wife.

THE LEOPARD IS JUST ONE OF THE 'BIG FIVE' SPOTTED AROUND SINGITA.

For more information
Singita Private Game Reserve
Sabi Sand Reserve
South Africa
T: +27 2168 33424
E: reservations@singita.co.za
www.singita.com

South Africa Tourism:
www.southafrica.net

The Icehotel,
Swedish Lapland

And the bride wore long johns. It may be corny, but a ceremony at the spectacular Ice Chapel in Swedish Lapland is enough to melt the coldest of hearts. At minus 6°C (21°F) inside, it comes as no surprise that some brides opt for cashmere and fleece socks, blue yeti boots (something blue, you understand), and thermal long johns, all set off by a garter over the top and a traditional white satin dress. Full-length fake fur coats are also popular, as are white ski suits with a veil. Fur muffs often take the place of a wedding bouquet, as flowers have a tough job coping with the temperature extremes (roses are the most resilient). Heated pocket warmers also come in handy before the exchange of rings.

Many couples head to the Icehotel and Chapel because they want to do something extraordinary, something memorable. And that's exactly what it delivers. Many bring family and friends to live the experience with them, as brides say it is so hard to describe just how weird and wonderful this venue is.

OPPOSITE: DIFFERENT ARTISTS AND ARCHITECTS REDESIGN THE ICE CHAPEL EACH YEAR.

BELOW: THERE IS AN AVERAGE OF 60 ROOMS THAT MAKE UP THE ICEHOTEL.

■ BEST TIME OF YEAR TO GO
The Icehotel and Chapel are usually open from 12 December until the spring thaw (usually mid-April).

■ CEREMONIES
Only religious ceremonies take place in the Ice Chapel. Civil ceremonies are available in the Icehotel, but most couples opt for the chapel.

■ PRE-WEDDING RESIDENCY
None required, but a visit to the registrar is necessary.

Situated on the bands of the Torne River, 200 km (125 miles) north of the Arctic Circle in the little village of Jukkasjärvi, which means 'meeting place', this yearly phenomenon is a unique creation by architects and artists. Their work lasts from around 12 December to mid-April, though it is of course at the mercy of the weather, and drips usually begin to appear around the end of April. More than 4,000 tonnes of ice and 30,000 cubic metres (40,000 cubic yards) of snow are used in the construction the Icehotel reception, hall of pillars, Iceart exhibition, Absolut Icebar, Icehotel cinema, and of course the Ice Chapel.

Couples must book well in advance for a wedding. All ceremonies that take place in the chapel are religious, with Christian symbols, and are conducted by the minister from Kiruna, 17 km (10 miles) away. Arrangements are tailormade with the help of the wedding coordinator, who requires good copies of the couple's birth certificates, passports, Superintendent Registrar's Non-Impediment to Marriage certificate (obtained from your local register office), and where necessary a decree absolute, ten to twelve weeks in advance of the wedding date. He or she forwards the papers to the Registration Bureau in Kiruna, where the paperwork is then prepared. When the couple arrive at the Icehotel, they are taken to meet the Registrar with all their original documents to formally sign an application and apply for a marriage licence. When couples marry on a working day (as they are obliged to at the Icehotel), the application and registration for a marriage licence can be issued on the same day as the ceremony.

Weddings here are held from Monday to Friday, and not at weekends. Many visitors understandably wonder whether they will be plunged into darkness in such a northerly location, but while it is true that the sun does not shine here at all during the last two weeks of the year, daylight gradually returns after this and the snow reflects all the light there is. Add to this the light from the myriad stars and the Northern Lights, which turn the sky pink or green, and the most doubtful sceptic would have to admit that there is a magical quality to the light here.

Since the Icehotel melts every spring to be rebuilt every winter, the exact number of rooms varies a little each year. On average there is a total of 60, including 32 double bedrooms, 20 ice suites, and two de luxe suites, in which newlyweds usually spend their wedding night. Each year a different artist is invited to sculpt these rooms around particular themes so no one year is the same as another. In the winter of 2004/5, one was based on the works of Leonardo da Vinci, with a portrayal of the Last Supper – in ice, of course – and the other had Manhattan as its inspiration, with a towering rendition of the iconic Chrysler Building beside the bed. These rooms are fairly spartan, as you would expect, containing little else but the block of ice that forms the bed, with a mattress and reindeer skins to lie on. Newlyweds snuggle up inside their double Arctic sleeping bag, often donning thermals and Sherpa hats to ward off the chill. Nevertheless, everyone who stays here swears that the experience is romantic. These are the only rooms with locks for extra privacy; in the morning a wake-up call comes in the form of the arrival of hot lingonberry juice: the Arctic conditions rule out breakfast in bed.

ABOVE: ICE BEDS ARE COVERED IN A MATTRESS AND REINDEER SKINS.

OPPOSITE: ROMANTIC SCULPTURES SET THE TONE FOR ICE WEDDINGS.

FIRE MEETS ICE INSIDE THE ICEHOTEL.

Most guests will actually sleep only one night in the Icehotel, spending the rest of their stay in the 'warm' part of the hotel. This consists of four-bed cabins; the two-bed Aurora Cabin, where you can lie in bed and watch the unreal colours of the Northern Lights through ceiling skylights; and rooms in the Kaamos Hotel. All these make perfect accommodation for wedding guests while the bride and groom spend their wedding night in the Icehotel itself.

The Chapel is constructed entirely of ice, including the altar and the font, with walls as high as 8 m (26 ft) and emitting a steely blue light. Indeed, this is as much a work of art as a chapel.

Although the design of the chapel changes every year, it always features the same spectacular ice chandelier. Fresh snow is brought in to dust the floor for a wedding. The ceremony usually lasts around 20 minutes and is conducted in Swedish, with the wedding coordinator translating. The priest may sing a hymn or two in Swedish, but there is often no other music. A local photographer can be booked to take pictures in the Ice Chapel, usually under the ice chandelier, or in the Absolut Icebar, or even in the couple's Ice Suite. A hairdresser and make-up artist can be brought in to prepare the bride, but many brides ask friends and family to help out.

A celebration vodka or Champagne in the Icebar is the thing to do after the ceremony. In the Absolut Icebar flavoured vodka shots are served 'in the rocks' rather than 'on the rocks', in ice glasses — most definitely the required tipple for entertaining guests. A plasma screen provides a live link to the Icebar in Stockholm, so newlyweds can show off their rings. There is also an Icebar in Milan and one due to open in London. The wedding breakfast is held in a choice of two 'warm' restaurants. Jukkasjärvi Wardshus serves gourmet Lapp cuisine, with raw fish from the Torne River served on plates of ice if desired, while the Old Homestead Restaurant offers local Swedish food. A typical wedding menu starts with whitefish roe (Swedish caviar) followed by roast reindeer, with cloudberry sorbet on ice for dessert. Rose petals and paper hearts are often scattered on the tables, and little glass baskets are filled with more rose petals and small ice sculptures such as hearts. Wedding cakes can be supplied, but some couples bring their own themed cake such as an igloo-shaped fruitcake.

The activities available around the Icehotel are a big draw for family and friends. As well as husky rides, these include snowmobiling, moose safaris, snowshoe trekking and reindeer sledding, and you can also try your hand at ice sculpting. There is a hot tub under the stars, and for those brave enough there is a sauna from which you can run out into minus 30°C (minus 22°F) to take a quick dip in a hole cut through the ice — not for the faint-hearted. One UK couple also took lottery tickets as a thank-you gift for all their guests, including in one envelope a ticket to go husky riding with the newlyweds the next day.

As those who have been there claim, the Icehotel is something that everyone should experience at least once in their lives. To hold your wedding here guarantees a memorable occasion, long johns and all.

For more information
Icehotel and Chapel
Jukkasjärvi
Swedish Lapland
T: +46 92066800
E: info@icehotel.com
www.icehotel.com

Swedish Tourist Board: www.visit-sweden.com
Discover the World (Arctic Experience):
www.discover-the-world.co.uk

Banyan Tree Phuket & the Chapel on the Lagoon, Thailand

Thailand is well known as a backpackers' paradise, an intriguing mix of the lurid back streets of Bangkok, hidden emerald lagoons and delicious castaway islands. Add to this a vibrant culture, gentle Thai hospitality and wonderful five-star resorts and spas, and you're starting to scratch the surface of what the 'land of smiles' has in store for couples in search of a serene wedding and honeymoon.

Phuket Island, on the jagged southwest coast of Thailand in the emerald Andaman Sea, has become a popular tourist destination, with its glistening white-sand beaches, coconut groves and sunny climate. Although Phuket was affected by the tsunami of Boxing Day 2004, the island's resorts are fully recovered and are extra-welcoming of visitors as tourism is what their livelihood relies on. Regular trips will take you out into Phang Nga Bay (where much of the James Bond film *The Man with the Golden Gun* was shot), with dramatic limestone karsts rising out of the water, covered in lush vegetation and hung with stalactites.

OPPOSITE: THE NON-DENOMINATIONAL CHAPEL ON THE LAGOON SEATS UP TO 50 GUESTS.

BELOW: THE CHAPEL IS INSPIRED BY THAILAND'S WATERBORNE CULTURE.

- **■ BEST TIME OF YEAR TO GO**
November to April (high season), May to September (low season).

- **■ CEREMONIES**
Religious, either Thai (Buddhist) or Western (Christian).

- **■ PRE-WEDDING RESIDENCY**
Three working days.

Phuket is usually blessed with good weather year-round. The hot (high) season runs from November to April and the rainy (low) season from May to September. Couples can therefore choose to come either during the tourist months from December to March, or in May, June and September, when it is less crowded.

For a marriage to be legally recognized under Thai law, the parties must be registered in the district Amphur, or Registrar's Office: in this case the Phuket Amphur. Foreigners must supply authenticated copies of their passport and a complete statutory declaration translated into Thai, and if they have been married before they must also have their original divorce certificate or the death certificate of their former spouse translated into Thai. These translated documents must be authenticated by the Legalization Division at the Ministry of Foreign Affairs in Bangkok. The whole process normally takes 48 hours. The couple must then return to the Amphur to register the marriage, after which they can marry at any register office or recognized place of marriage in Thailand, such as the Chapel on the Lagoon. The Banyan Tree's on-site wedding coordinators will help arrange all these legal details.

Set on the shores of Bang Tao Bay, Banyan Tree Phuket is one of the most beautiful and romantic hotels on the island, part of Laguna Phuket, Asia's first integrated resort. There are five luxury resorts and six palm-fringed lagoons, 600 acres of parkland and 3 km (1.8 miles) of pristine beach to enjoy. As the resorts lie side by side, visitors have the advantage of being able to use facilities at all five resorts.

Couples wishing to tie the knot somewhere other than the beach need look no further than the stunning new Chapel on the Lagoon, available exclusively to guests at Laguna Phuket. Inspired by Thailand's waterborne culture, this charming white-painted wooden structure with glass walls seems to float on the water, though in fact it is supported on stilts. Its pitched roof and pavilion-style decks pay homage to traditional Thai architecture, while its glass sliding doors can be opened to create an alfresco ceremony. The airy interior has an atmosphere of reverence, and the panoramic 360-degree views of the lagoon impart a feeling of union with nature — at sunset it is magical.

The nondenominational chapel seats up to 50 guests comfortably on beautifully covered white chairs, often decorated with simple golden bows. For more intimate weddings, some seating can be removed and a cosier arrangement laid out inside. Western (Christian) or Thai (Buddhist) ceremonies can be held. Thai weddings feature blessings by Buddhist monks and Thai musicians and attendants in traditional costumes; couples may even opt to have an elephant grace their big day. If they prefer their own music to Thai musicians, there is a Bose sound system or a traditional church organ to grant their wishes.

The bride arrives by water on a traditional long-tailed boat named Sanya Rak, meaning 'Promise of Love'. The chapel has rest rooms with a full-length mirror so she can check her appearance before walking down the aisle. A framed 'Welcome' notice board in the entrance to the chapel allows the bride and groom to display a personalized greeting to all their guests.

LEFT: CHOOSE BETWEEN THAI GARLANDS OR WESTERN STYLE FLOWERS.

RIGHT: PHANG NGA BAY WITH ITS DRAMATIC LIMESTONE KARSTS.

Once the cake has been cut and the Champagne served after the ceremony, all the guests can be ferried to the reception venue at the Banyan Tree Phuket by boat.

For just the two of you, or perhaps with a couple of friends, the Sanya Rak dinner cruise makes a memorable nuptial celebration. The boat is staffed by your own host, chef and traditional Thai musician, and with only one cruise on the lagoon in the evening there is no risk of bumping into other couples. The choice of five menus includes Western, two Thai menus and two vegetarian options. The Thai menu includes classic dishes such as tom kha gai (chicken and coconut soup with lime) and kao suay

(steamed jasmine rice). Truffles and pralines finish off the meal, or of course wedding cake and Champagne.

Couples who want an intimate dining experience in the privacy of their villa can enjoy a barbecue for two under the stars in their villa garden on their poolside terrace. A chef will come and prepare delicious dishes. Midnight feasts or Champagne breakfasts are also available. If a more formal reception is required, there is a selection of restaurants to choose from at the Banyan Tree Phuket, including the superb Saffron, which serves Asian dishes with exotic twists such as crisp fried catfish with mango salad, sticky rice and curry ice cream.

Another option is the Tamarind, a semi-alfresco restaurant beside the pool offering fresh fish and light meals.

After the wedding celebrations, couples return to their villa to find their bed swathed in midnight-blue Thai silk and petals, with incense and candles burning gently. There is also a candlelit outdoor bath overflowing with orchid petals and a bottle of bubbly on ice. Even the resident frogs seem loved up and full of Thai goodwill.

The Banyan Tree Phuket's spa pool villas are highly recommended for honeymooners. We are not talking plunge pools here rather; a very swimmable green-tiled pool surrounded by ornamental statues, double sunbathing loungers, chic tented pavilions and private terrace for meals under the stars. On arrival, all five senses are set tingling with the aromatic fragrances of incense and aromatherapy oils, soft background music and the beautiful decoration of the villas. Among the delights here is the 'floating bed pavilion': a glass-walled bedroom set over a tranquil lily pond, where you can choose Thai silk sheets and select the consistency of the pillows for the king-size bed from a 'pillow menu'. Above is a high, draped ceiling resembling a grand Mongolian canopy, which sways gently in the breeze. One of the wonderful things about the spa pool villas is that they are completely private: newlyweds can enjoy an outdoor shower together amid tropical greenery, bask naked on the sundecks without inhibition or lounge unobserved on the luxurious sheets of their pavilion bed, admiring the pink water lilies floating around them.

Several visits to the spa before and after the wedding are an absolute must. Banyan Tree Phuket has been voted the World's Best Spa Resort by readers of the prestigious *Condé Nast Traveller* magazine, and its outdoor stone-built double treatment rooms resemble mini-temples, with goldfish- and lily-filled water inlets and sensuous massages, wraps, rubs, scrubs, facials, steam healers and herbal baths that draw on ancient Asian traditions. A pampering two-hour rejuvenation spa package is usually offered to newlyweds. Alternatively, intimate tailormade spa packages can be enjoyed in the pavilion of the couple's spa pool villa garden, with side-by-side massage beds. A bridal beauty package includes a manicure, pedicure and facial treatment, ensuring brides look radiant on their big day.

With such a strong sense of Thai culture from the waterborne chapel to the long-tailed boat, couples are assured of memorable day, infused with a great sense of place.

ABOVE TOP: PRIVATE POOLS OFFER
TOTAL PRIVACY.

ABOVE: BLUE THAI SILK SHEETS AND
FRANGIPANI BLOOMS ON YOUR
WEDDING NIGHT.

For more information
Banyan Tree Phuket
33 Moo 4, Srisoonthorn Road, Cherngtalay
Amphur Talang, Phuket 83110, Thailand
T: +66 7632 4374
E: phuket@banyantree.com   www.banyantree.com

Chapel on the Lagoon: T: +66 7632 4060
www.lagunaphuketweddings.com

Tourism Authority of Thailand: www.thaismile.co.uk

The Venetian,
Las Vegas, USA

Elvis and Priscilla did it. Bruce and Demi, Cindy and Richard, Billy Bob and Angelina all did it. Getting hitched in the City of Sin is still the height of wedding kitsch. Even Britney tied the knot here, then got her divorce papers as quickly as she said 'I do'. This vast metropolis of lights in the Nevada Desert has carved out a reputation as the wedding capital of the world. In this home of kiss-me-quick vows, more than 120,000 marriage licences are issued annually, equivalent to almost half the number of marriages that take place throughout the whole of Britain in a year. The process is as easy as saying 'I do', and the venue can be as tacky or classy as you wish.

Las Vegas is legendary for its weddings at the Little White Chapel. Couples can have an Elvis lookalike presiding over a 24-hour drive-through wedding, or take their vows while bungee jumping. If you want a *Star Trek* theme, this is the place for you. Daredevil couples have even said 'I do' in a helicopter hovering over the nearby Grand Canyon. Many chapels offer live Internet coverage, so absent family and friends can watch the exchange of vows. This is a great city to bring a group of lively friends to for a wedding, while still retaining its image as the place to which to run away together for a spur-of-the-moment wedding.

OPPOSITE: THE VENETIAN TYPIFIES THE MAKE-BELIEVE MENTALITY OF LAS VEGAS.

BELOW: KISS ME QUICK VOWS IN DOWNTOWN VEGAS.

■ BEST TIME OF YEAR TO GO
The weather is best in April, May and June. New Year's Eve and Valentine's Day are the most popular days for weddings, and for these it is necessary to book well in advance. Since the Millennium, couples have been attracted by memorable wedding dates such as 1/01/01, 2/02/02 and so on.

■ CEREMONIES
Nondenominational religious.

■ PRE-WEDDING RESIDENCY
None — this is the home of kiss-me-quick vows.

There are no residency requirements for marrying in Las Vegas, but a marriage licence is necessary. Both the future bride and groom must pay a visit to the Marriage License Bureau at 200 South Third Street in downtown Las Vegas. The office is open from 8 am until midnight on weekdays and from 8 am on Friday until midnight on Sunday every weekend. It is also open 24 hours on holidays. Even with those opening hours there are still queues. Couples must present some form of identification and proof of age, such as passports or birth certificates, and a decree absolute if divorced, clearly indicating the date and place that the decree was registered. They must hand over US$55 in cash, and once they have their licence anyone licensed to perform ceremonies in the state of Nevada

can perform their marriage ceremony, which must take place within one year of the date their licence is issued. After the ceremony couples will be presented with a proof of marriage certificate. Couples must then register their marriage either in the UK at their local town hall, or in the State of Nevada. To register in Nevada, couples must take their proof of marriage certificate to the license office and purchase an official marriage certificate for $10.

Over the past ten years, Las Vegas has shed some of its seedy gambling image in favour of an adult theme-park approach, with a profusion of world-class restaurants and spas adding to the mix. Some of the themed hotels include New York, New York, where you can wed on a rollercoaster; Excalibur in medieval costumes; and Treasure Island, where pirates are the required look. A new push to be taken seriously as a purveyor of the arts was marked by the Bellagio Hotel's advertisement for its Monets, Renoirs and Picassos in lights on the Strip, just like a Broadway show. In its centenary year — celebrating when Las Vegas was born on 15 May 1905 when 110 acres of land were auctioned by the rail road — 2005 saw 100 weddings held on the day itself, and Las Vegas celebrated the opening of the US$2.7 billion Wynn Las Vegas resort, with no fewer than 2,700 rooms. Steve Wynn, its billionaire developer, claims that it is the most expensive hotel to be built in North America and will inject class and refinement — despite its 2,000 blinking 'Slots A Fun' fruit machines. A major draw of Las Vegas is its proximity to the Grand Canyon. An incredible glass Skywalk opens in 2006 and couples can choose to tie the knot suspended above the Grand Canyon. (See: www.destinationgrandcanyon.com and 'Skywalk'.)

The Venetian, developed by Sheldon Adelson, was modelled after the great Italian city on water, and is perhaps the most outrageous example of the make-believe mentality of Las Vegas. This 4,000-room giant of a hotel offers a sanitized version of the Venetian 'experience', without the troublesome crumbling façades and flooded piazzas. A wedding at the Venetian would appeal to couples looking for a gloriously fun and irreverent occasion. The surreal juxtaposition of a fake Campanile with a multistorey hotel behind is a sight to behold. The hotel takes its weddings deadly seriously and can provide all the traditional trimmings, from rose bouquets to Champagne, though couples should be prepared to revel in the ridiculous. What could be more wonderfully tacky than getting married in a fake gondola on a fake Grand Canal, under a painted sky in a grandiose building just off the famous Vegas Strip?

All ceremonies here are performed by state licensed celebrants of a religious affiliation, though they are nondenominational and with no religious content unless requested. Rabbis and chuppahs are available for Jewish weddings. The hotel offers a choice of three wedding venues: on a gondola, on the bridge, or in the hotel chapel. In the heart of the hotel is a

THERE'S NO UNDERESTIMATING THE
OPULENCE AT THE VENETIAN.

painstaking replica of the Grand Canal, with
a white gondola specially for weddings.
The bride and groom are serenaded by a
'gondolier' in striped T-shirt and straw
boater. The bridge in question is the Ponte
al di Piazza, or the Bridge over the Square'
modelled on the famous Rialto bridge in
Venice. Even if you don't have your ceremony
at either of these locations, a photo call in
either or both is a must. Couples drape
themselves over the bridge with the 'Artisti
del Arte' —street performers and Italian opera
singers — supplied by the hotel to provide
local colour. These two venues are perfect
for intimate weddings à deux. For larger, more
traditional weddings, the Venetian Wedding
Chapel, overlooking the pool deck and lush
gardens, has seated accommodation for 150,
or can be partitioned to take up to 50 guests.

Couples should be prepared to see many
other wedding couples on their big day.
This is Vegas, after all. A Venetian Event
Planner will take couples through all the
arrangements, and for a spur-of-the-moment
occasion can even steer them in the
direction of wedding gown stores or rentals.

In addition to the six wedding packages available, individual requests are also catered for. The most basic package is the 'Cerimonia Sul' Aqua' ('Ceremony on Water'), which includes a ceremony in the white gondola, a customized bouquet and groom's boutonnière (buttonhole), and two digital prints. At the top end is the 'Fortuna' (Good Fortune) package, which offers everything from 92 prints and a one-hour video to a 30-minute rehearsal, Perrier Jouet champagne gift set, chocolate tuxedo strawberries, breakfast in bed, suite upgrade, Canyon Ranch SpaClub day-pass for two with massages or Rasul (a mud bath and rain shower for two), and a bridal salon package of hair, manicure and pedicure.

Once vows have been exchanged, wedding parties can enjoy a Champagne toast against a backdrop of a stately fountain or on a private outdoor patio overlooking an intimate courtyard of statues and flowers. Wedding breakfasts can be held in a choice of 12 restaurants, some with celebrity restaurateurs at the helm, such as Wolfgang Puck's Postrio and Kevin Wu's Royal Star. A flautist, guitarist, jazz trio or even a classical Italian opera singer can accompany the reception, while a magician or juggler works the tables. Everything from rose petals strewn in the path of the bride and groom to disposable cameras and stardust on the tables can be arranged. Ice carvings such as wedding bells or interlocking rings with the initials of the bride and groom are popular, and very Vegas. But perhaps the height of Vegas kitsch is the wedding cake. Master pastry chef Peter Wimmler creates cakes topped with virtually anything, from flowers spilling from an antique floral teacup that matches the couple's own china to a model of The Venetian itself. The secret of marrying in Las Vegas is to revel in the over-the-top nature of it all. So jump in that superstretch limo and enjoy!

For more information
The Venetian
3355 Las Vegas Boulevard South
Las Vegas, Nevada 89109, USA
T: +1 866 548 1807
E: weddings@venetian.com
www.venetian.com

Las Vegas Convention & Visitors Authority:
www.visitlasvegas.co.uk
or call 0870-823 8832 for a free guide

Four Seasons Hotel, New York, USA

The Big Apple is synonymous with romance, from *West Side Story* (an updated *Romeo and Juliet*) to *When Harry Met Sally*. From horse-and-carriage rides à deux around Central Park to a little something from Tiffany's in one of those must-have turquoise boxes, there's a constant buzz about the Big Apple.

Ask anyone what Manhattan brings to mind, and that tumultuous skyline has to come out tops. Skyscrapers make Manhattan the majestic city it is. They are a symbol of defiance, of pushing boundaries, of that most American of attributes — reaching for the stars. The Four Seasons New York is the tallest hotel in Manhattan, and pays homage to the giants of the city that date back to the art deco era of the 1920s: the Empire State Building, the Rockefeller Building and the Chrysler Building.

The architect who designed the Four Seasons is I. M. Pei, creator of the famous glass pyramid in the courtyard of the Louvre in Paris. Just as that echoes Napoleon's love of ancient Egypt, so his design for the Four Seasons New York harks back to a golden age of towering monuments that confidently symbolized America as the most powerful country in the world.

OPPOSITE: THE FOUR SEASONS NEW YORK IS THE TALLEST HOTEL IN THE CITY.

BELOW: THE DRAMA OF MANHATTAN BEFITS A SPECIAL OCCASION.

- ■ **BEST TIME OF YEAR TO GO**
  October and November are most spectacular for the fall foliage.

- ■ **CEREMONIES**
  Civil or religious.

- ■ **PRE-WEDDING RESIDENCY**
  One day.

New Yorkers recommend fall, or autumn, as the best time of year to marry in the city. The Four Seasons is located just blocks from Central Park, and in November the trees are ablaze with colour, making a picture-perfect setting. It also falls neatly between the hot summer months and the hectic winter season.

Couples dreaming of a bold venue should look no further than this soaring hotel that makes no secret of its ambition to be the best. This graceful limestone spire, built in 1993, soars high above its near-perfect location between Madison and Park Avenues, just a few steps away from Central Park. Its 52 storeys were the most costly to construct of any building in the city, with each room racking up a bill of around US$1 million (£550,000).

On entering the hotel for the first time, the lobby is a revelation. You are immediately overawed by the spectacular onyx ceiling that soars 10 m (33 feet) above the entrance hall, designed to be one of New York's grandest indoor public spaces. Outsized art deco-style torches light the stairway to the lobby. The hotel's artwork features signed prints by Le Corbusier, Magritte and Kandinsky. The romance here is palpable, and the knowledgeable concierge receives numerous requests to help arrange spectacular wedding proposals, such as private helicopter trips over the Statue of Liberty or horse-and-carriage rides around Central Park.

To obtain a marriage licence, couples must apply in person to any town or city clerk in the state of New York. The application for a licence must be signed by both the bride and groom in the presence of the town or city clerk, so a representative cannot apply for the licence on their behalf. The marriage licence is issued immediately, but the marriage ceremony may not take place within 24 hours of the exact time when the licence was issued.

LEFT: FIVE STAR WEDDING DETAILS AT THE FOUR SEASONS.

RIGHT: DINNER AND DANCING FOR UP TO 100 IN THE COSMOPOLITAN SUITE.

OPPOSITE: THE SOARING LOBBY WAS BUILT TO IMPRESS.

There is no particular form required in the ceremony, except that the parties must state in the presence of an authorized member of the clergy or public official and at least one other witness that they take one another as husband and wife. The person performing the ceremony must be registered with the City of New York in order to perform a wedding within the New York City limits.

Couples can marry at the Four Seasons, of course, but if they prefer to have a church wedding before a reception at the hotel, these are usually held at the church of St Bartholomew on Park Avenue and 50th Street or St Ignatius Loyola on Park Avenue and 84th Street. Horse-drawn carriages to and from the hotel and photographs in nearby Central Park are some of the typical New York touches that couples may expect.

Those who choose to wed at the Four Seasons New York generally have the ceremony in the Metropolitan Suite,

followed by cocktails in the Metropolitan foyer and dinner and dancing for up to 100 people in the Cosmopolitan Suite. This majestic room reflects the signature decor of the hotel lobby, with walls panelled in light beech making the perfect complement to the floral table decorations. The Four Seasons New York is not a 'ballroom' hotel, unlike many of its rivals, but rather specializes in smaller weddings (with 60 to 100 guests) in a more intimate, elegant style.

Couples who marry at the hotel spend their wedding night in a complimentary Four Seasons Executive Suite, where a bottle of Veuve Clicquot and chocolate-covered strawberries await them. The rooms have ultra-romantic views of Central Park, sycamore-panelled dressing rooms and marble bathrooms with steeping tubs that fill in 60 seconds, some with stunning views of Manhattan. All the rooms are large by city standards.

I. M. Pei emerged from retirement to design two new suites that opened in 2005. These transparent penthouses high in the sky have their own log fireplaces and enjoy breathtaking views from the Hudson to the East River. Floor to ceiling bay windows were designed to make guests feel they are floating above the city. Outside balconies are positioned on the corners of the building to give a diagonal view of Manhattan, 51 floors above Madison Avenue. Central Park appears to be within touching distance and the New York skyline is laid out before you. Priced at US$15,000 (£8,200) a night, these iconic suites claim to be the most expensive in America outside gaming properties. The interiors of the suites are by the flamboyant architect Peter Marino, who designed the Louis Vuitton store next door, and who has spared no expense in his use of delicate fabrics and white carpets. Each suite creates a different atmosphere and is quite unique; Suite 5101 suggests an opulent, masculine library, while Suite 5102 seems to hum with the vibrancy of a sophisticated cocktail party with cream-coloured credenzas, customized games tables and a baby grand piano. Carrie Bradshaw eat your heart out!

ABOVE TOP: PENTHOUSE SUITES HAVE PANORAMIC VIEWS ACROSS MANHATTAN.

ABOVE: VEUVE CLICQUOT CHAMPAGNE AWAITS NEWLYWEDS IN THEIR SUITE.

The Four Seasons has an on-site wedding expert who will work with couples to reserve dates, plan the schedule of events and coordinate all food and drinks, from menu designs to linens. They will also assist with the legal paperwork. A florist, or 'floral designer' as they are known in Manhattan, is available on request, a customized wedding cake can be created by the talented in-house pastry chef, and everything from an intimate family brunch to a sophisticated cocktail buffet or grand reception banquet can be arranged. One option you might like to try for the wedding breakfast is a 'Tasting Menu', a meal designed as five to eight courses in tasting portions, paired with the appropriate wines and champagne. The Fifty Seven Fifty Seven Restaurant, which serves stylish American cuisine, has been awarded an unprecedented three-star rating by the *New York Times*, while the adjacent bar has one of the best buzzes in the city and is famous for its citrus martinis.

Brides-to-be can pamper themselves in the spa before the wedding and chill out there afterwards. As well as New Wave treatments such as Inner Pulse Light Therapy, the spa also offers more mainstream manicures and pedicures, as well as wedding hair and make-up. All the spa treatments are also available for men, of course, and the groom may like to prepare for the wedding with a traditional steam-towel shave featuring products from London's famous barbers Geo F. Trumper.

In the winter months, couples who are real chocoholics can book the Chocolate Package, which features a chocolate bar in their room serving chocolate martinis, homemade chocolate bars and chocolate-covered strawberries. You can even snuggle down for the night and watch films from the complimentary DVD library including *Chocolat*, *Like Water for Chocolate* and *Willy Wonka and the Chocolate Factory* !

And for those who live to shop, there's even a 24-hour shopping service at Bergdorf Goodman in case you've forgotten a vital something on the eve of your wedding day, or just fancy indulging one another.

For honeymooners, New York is a honeypot of delights. As well as the tried and tested attractions of Central Park, Fifth Avenue, Greenwich Village and Soho, there are the uber trendy areas to explore such as the Meatpacking District with its cutting edge bars, restaurants, and clubs from the rooftop pool at Soho House to the faux Parisian chic of Pastis. As the song goes, 'New York, New York, so good they named it twice...'

STOP AT TIFFANY & CO FOR THE
WEDDINGS RINGS OR A SPECIAL
KEEPSAKE OF THE BIG DAY.

For more information
Four Seasons New York
57 East 57th Street
New York NY 10022, USA
T: +1 212 7585700
E: res.fsnewyork@fourseasons.com
www.fourseasons.com

New York Tourism:
www.nycvisit.com

Contact details for all resorts featured
in this book:

Anassa Resort
P.O. Box 66006
8830 Polis
Cyprus
T: +357 268 88000
E: gserv.anassa@thanoshotels.com
www.thanoshotels.com

Ashford Castle
Cong, Co. Mayo
Ireland
T: +353 92 46003
E: banqueting@ashford.ie
www.ashford.ie

Banyan Tree Phuket
33 Moo 4, Srisoonthorn Road
Cherngtalay
Amphur Talang
Phuket 83110
Thailand
T: +66 7632 4374
E: phuket@banyantree.com
www.banyantree.com

Hotel Budir
Budir, Snaefellsnes
356 Snaefellsbaer
Iceland
T: +354 435 6700
E: ulli@budir.is
www.budir.is

Cap Juluca
Maundays Bay
Anguilla
British West Indies
T: +1 264 4976779
E: info@capjuluca.com
www.capjuluca.com

Château de Bagnols
69620 Bagnols
France
T: +33 474 714000
E: info@bagnols.com
www.roccofortehotels.com

Hotel Cipriani & Palazzo Vendramin
Giudecca 10
30133 Venice
Italy
T: +39 041 5207744
E: info@hotelcipriani.it
www.hotelcipriani.com

Fairmont Banff Springs
405 Spray Avenue
Banff
Alberta
Canada
T: +1 403 762 2211
E: banffsprings@fairmont.com
www.fairmont.com/banffsprings

Four Seasons New York
57 East 57th Street
New York
NY 10022
USA
T: +1 212 758 5700
E: res.fsnewyork@fourseasons.com
www.fourseasons.com

Frégate Island Private
Seychelles
T: 00 248 670 100
E: info@fregate.com
www.fregate.com

The Grove
Chandler's Cross
Hertfordshire
UK
T: +44 (0)1923 807807
E: info@thegrove.co.uk
www.thegrove.co.uk

Hayman
Great Barrier Reef
Queensland
4801 Australia
T: +61 7494 01681
E: mtarry@hayman.com.au
www.hayman.com.au

Icehotel and Chapel

Jukkasjärvi

Swedish Lapland

T: +46 92066800

E: info@icehotel.com

www.icehotel.com

Necker Island

Limited Edition by Virgin

Voyager House

5 The Lanchesters

162–164 Fulham Palace Road

London W6 9ER

UK

T: +44 (0)20 8600 0430 (UK and France);

T: +1 732 473 9982 (US)

E: enquiries@limitededition.virgin.co.uk

www.neckerisland.com

The Oberoi Rajvilas

Goner Road

Jaipur

Rajasthan 30301

India

T: +91 1412 68 0101

E: gm@oberoi-rajvilas.com

www.oberoihotels.com

One&Only Palmilla

Los Cabos

Mexico

T: +52 624 146 7000

E: reservations@oneandonlypalmilla.com

www.oneandonlypalmilla.com

Pangkor Laut Resort

Pangkor Laut Island

32200 Lumut Perak

Malaysia

T: +800 9899 9999

E: travelcentre@ytlhotels.com.my

www.pangkorlaut.com

The Peninsula Hong Kong

Salisbury Road

Kowloon

Hong Kong

T: +852 2920 2888

E: pen@peninsula.com

www.peninsula.com

Prestonfield House

Prestonfield Road

Edinburgh

Scotland EH16 5UT

UK

T: +44 (0)131 225 7800

E: weddings@prestonfield.com

www.prestonfield.com

Raffles Resort Canouan Island

St Vincent & The Grenadines

West Indies

T: +1 784 4588000

E: info@raffles-canouanisland.com

www.raffles-canouanisland.com

Singita Private Game Reserve

Sabi Sand Reserve

South Africa

T: +27 2168 33424

E: reservations@singita.co.za

www.singita.com

Vatulele Island Resort

Fiji

T: +679 672 0300

E: res@vatulele.com

www.vatulele.com

The Venetian

3355 Las Vegas Boulevard South

Las Vegas

Nevada 89109

USA

T: +1 866 548 1807

E: weddings@venetian.com

www.venetian.com

Villa San Michele

Via Doccia 4

Fiesole

50014 Florence

Italy

T: +39 055 5678200

E: reservations@villasanmichele.net

www.villasanmichele.com

Voile d'Or Resort and Spa

Bel Ombre

Mauritius

T: +230 466 1900

E: info@voiledor.com

www.voiledor.com

Picture credits

The publisher would like to thank the following photographers, agencies, resorts and venues for their kind permission to reproduce the photographs in this book:

4–5 National Magazines/Retna UK; 6 Laguna Phuket, Thailand; 8–10 Cap Juluca, Anguilla; 11 Peter Casolino/Alamy; 12–13 Cap Juluca, Anguilla; 14 Hayman Island Resort; 15 Tourism Queensland; 16–19 Hayman Island Resort; 20–21 Halpern Ltd/Necker Island; 22–23 Virgin Limited Edition/Necker Island; 24–25 Halpern Ltd/Necker Island; 26 Bonner Photography; 27 Fairmont Banff Springs; 28 Bonner Photography; 29 left Fairmont Banff Springs; 29 right Bonner Photography; 30–31 Fairmont Banff Springs; 32–37 The Anassa, Cyprus; 38–43 The Grove, Hertfordshire; 44–47 Courtesy of Vatulele Island Resort; 48 Vatulele Island Resort/Courtesy of Turquoise Holidays; 49 Courtesy of Vatulele Island Resort; 50–54 Marcus Lyon for Rocco Forte Hotels; 55 Images of France; 56–59 Studio Livio; 60 Chris Caldicott; 61 above Studio Livio; 61 below Chris Caldicott; 62–64 above The Peninsula, Hong Kong; 64 below David Sanger/Alamy; 65 The Peninsula, Hong Kong; 66–67 Hong Kong Tourist Board; 68 Elisa Locci/Alamy; 69–71 Hotel Budir; 72–73 Ragnar Sigurdsson/Arctic Images; 74–77 Oberoi Rajvilas/Ann Scott Associates; 78 John Warburton-Lee Photography; 79 M.Garrett/ Robert Harding; 80–81 Andrew Holt/Alamy; 82 above Zefa/Grace; 82 below–84 Ashford Castle; 85 Chris Hill/Scenic Ireland; 86 Andre Jenny/Alamy; 87–91 Genivs Loci/Orient Express Hotels; 92–94 Orient Express Hotels; 95 above Craig Wilson/Travel Ink; 95 below Antony Nagelmann/Getty Images;

96–97 Orient Express Hotels; 98–99 Pangkor Laut Resort; 100–101 Orson Liyu/Pangkor Laut Resort; 102–103 Pangkor Laut Resort; 104–109 Fotoseeker; 110-115 One&Only Resorts; 116–119 above Prestonfield, Edinburgh; 119 below Adrian Houston; 120-121 Prestonfield, Edinburgh; 122–127 Frégate Island Private, Seychelles; 128–133 Singita Private Game Reserve; 134–135 Mark Luscombe-Whyte/Elizabeth Whiting and Associates; 136 Peter Grant Photography; 137 Elisa Locci/Alamy; 138 Chad Ehlers/Alamy; 139 Mark Luscombe-Whyte/Elizabeth Whiting and Associates; 140–143 left Laguna Phuket, Thailand; 143 right Narratives; 144–145 Laguna Phuket, Thailand; 146 Richard Cummins/Corbis; 147 ImageState/Alamy; 148 left Las Vegas News Bureau/Cellet PR, London; 148 right–149 Courtesy of the Venetian, Las Vegas; 150 Las Vegas News Bureau/Cellet PR, London; 151 Sundance Helicopters; 152 Four Seasons Hotels and Resorts; 153 Microzoa/Getty Images; 154 left–156 Four Seasons Hotels and Resorts; 157 Kevin Foy/Alamy.

Every effort has been made to trace the images' copyright holders. We apologise in advance for any unintentional omissions, and would be pleased to insert the appropriate acknowledgment in any subsequent printing.

The author would like to thank:

Carolyn Altieri, Claire Appleby, Antonia Bristowe, Hamish Buchanan, Lucinda Buxton, Kate Chesshyre, Lucy Chisholm, Joanne Cochrane, Andrea Daunt, Fiona Duthie, Monica Feeney, Lucy Flemming, Elena Giorgetti, Naomi Graham, Sian Griffiths, Carole Hamilton, Sue Heady , Georgina Hancock, Susie Hanbury, Vicky Hubbard, Melanie Jones, Vicky Legg, Katy Lamb, Leanne Loots, Fiona Lovett, Sally Morgan, Julia Record, Sue Reitz, Verna Rogers, Mark Rowley, Emma Salvadori, Antje Schellenberg, Kate Smallwood, George Sotelo, Carly Smith, Monica Tarry, Ulfar Thordarson, Steve Tooze, Andrea Wait, Jane West and the team at Conran Octopus.